D1565850

THE GODS

THE *Gods*

Albert Goldbarth

OHIO STATE UNIVERSITY PRESS

Columbus

Copyright © 1993 by the Ohio State University Press.
All rights reserved.

Library of Congress Cataloging-in-Publication Data

Goldbarth, Albert.
    The gods / Albert Goldbarth.
       p.   cm.
    ISBN 0–8142–0595–X. — ISBN 0–8142–0596–8 (pbk.)
    I. Title.
    PS3557.0354G6   1992
    811'.54—dc20   92–18713
                                                              CIP

Text and jacket design by Bruce Gore, Gore Studio, Inc.
Type set in Weiss by Focus Graphics, St. Louis, Missouri.
Printed by Braun-Brumfield, Inc., Ann Arbor, Michigan.

The paper in this book meets the guidelines for permanence and durability
of the Committee on Production Guidelines for Book Longevity of the
Council on Library Resources.

9   8   7   6   5   4   3   2

ACKNOWLEDGMENTS

My thanks to the editors of the following journals,
where the poems of *The Gods* first appeared,
sometimes in earlier versions.

The Beloit Poetry Journal: Lullabye

Crazyhorse: Shoyn Fergéssin: "I've Forgotten" in Yiddish

The Denver Quarterly: The Jewish Poets of Arabic Spain (10th to 13th Centuries), with Chinese Poets Piping Out of Clouds (and Once an Irishman)

The Georgia Review: 16th Century, Brush and Ink: *A Hermit on a Riverbank;* Will the Real Shakespeare Please Stand Up?; The Voices

The Indiana Review: 1563; A Refuge

The Journal: Adventures in Decipherment

The Laurel Review: The Books / P, L, E; Would you know a Snook, or a Large-eyed Whiff, from a Goggle-eyed Scad, should the necessity arise? . . . I thought so.; Sill Ritual: a survey

The Ohio Review: The Flowers of Koonwarra

The Ontario Review: Sumerian Votive Figurines; Gallery; A World Above Suffering

ONTHEBUS: How Easy It Is; The Two Parts of the Day Are,

Parnassus: Not to Contravene

Poetry: "When wild beasts charge,; The Title for a Collection of Poems Appears from Out of Nowhere; Alveoli

Poetry East: Architectural

Poetry Northwest: Thermodynamics / Sumer

Southwest Review: A Pantheon

TriQuarterly: The Gold Note Lounge and Boogie Palace

The Virginia Quarterly Review: Stories

Enter ALBERT
Albert.   Good Gods!

John Keats (from *Otho the Great*)

CONTENTS

Sumerian Votive Figurines 1

My People
1: The Mythic Adventures of Louie and Rosie 5

Shoyn Fergéssin: "I've Forgotten" in Yiddish 7
1563 8
Gallery 12
The Flowers of Koonwarra 14
A World Above Suffering 17
The Story of Dorsett 22
The Jewish Poets of Arabic Spain (10th to 13th Centuries), with Chinese
    Poets Piping Out of Clouds (and Once an Irishman) 26

My People
2: Marriage in Translation 37

The Books / P, L, E 39
Thermodynamics / Sumer 47
16th Century, Brush and Ink: *A Hermit on a Riverbank* 48
Would you know a Snook, or a Large-eyed Whiff, from a Goggle-eyed
    Scad, should the necessity arise? . . . I thought so. 50
How Easy It Is 52
Will the Real Shakespeare Please Stand Up? 54

Sill Ritual: a survey   56
"When wild beasts charge,   59
The Title for a Collection of Poems Appears from Out of Nowhere   62
Adventures in Decipherment   64
The Two Parts of the Day Are,   69

Adonai and Company   71

The Gold Note Lounge and Boogie Palace   73
A Pantheon   75
A Refuge   78
Alveoli   81
Stories   83
Thawed   85
Not to Contravene   87
Architectural   92
The Voices   93

The Book of Speedy   99

Lullabye   121

Notes   125

Sumerian Votive Figurines

Sumerian Votive Figurines

were meant to pray, unceasingly, on their owners' behalves.
He thinks: they still might, even though the proper recipient
gods have long since gone to theology mulch; this faith is
stone and for the most part unbroken. Choired-up
this way—there's an even dozen he's studying—something
hushed and intercessionary *does* texture the air in a circle
around their geometricized devotional posture. Some were done
300 years apart, and yet a gentle uniformity attends these
stand-in men and women; he thinks of his own
world's fashions of 300 years ago, then shakes his head, because
what kind of halfass world-class Sumerologist *is* he, dizzy
at the edge of cracked conjecture when he should be adding up facts?
In any case, it's lunchtime: baloney-and-curry on white with
chocolate cream-filled Ooh-Oohs for dessert, and the mail is letters
from both of his kids. He shakes his head again, he needs to: Lou, poor
Lou, was nabbed two years ago by the FBI for harboring a stolen
circus elephant (the poop of which contained ten bags
of paradise-quality coke, though Lou persuasively argued ignorance),
    then
Becky (spouses always sensing the moment of thinnest defense
in one another) left on the day of his trial, left with someone
who styled himself (or so the script across the leather jacket blared)
The King of Venusian Blues, whatever that was (or wherever). Melanie,
meanwhile, couldn't be more jet-propelled successful; every week,
it seems, her company ("The Company," she says, like "Truth" or
    "Eternity")
eats some smaller companyette, and while she once was Lord Almighty
of its Alabama xerox network, now she oversees
the "coastal-corridor/Europe conglomerate" for an empire of
"communications outreach" where, so far as he can tell from what
she patiently details, you can press a button in DC and, *whoosh*,

two blueprints, a bundle of money the size of a basketball, and, if
you want, a troupe of lubriciously spangled naiads tumbles
from a cloud of hi-tech pixie dust into a boardroom in Rome.
There are photos, from each, of the grandkids: Sonny
sporting a t-shirt tricked up with an airbrushed skull on fire
vomiting various barnyard animals; and Darlene
in a ballerina's tutu making her porky 4-year-old's body
look, he'd swear, as if it just passed a very diaphanous fart.
It could make a man—what? guffaw? weep? or
see it's 5 P.M. by now and shake his head, and grab his lunchbox
(painted by Estelle to be an Assyrian sphinx) and head home.
Each day, five days a week, for seven years, he's exited this freeway
at BUBBA'S LAWN ORNAMENTS PAINTED OR PLAIN, and
nodded at the plaster hundreds grouped below its awning: gnomes
(whose bases reveal they're Lumpy, Dumpy, and Frumpy), fawns
and bucks, a contingent of Venus de Milos and several representatives
from the world of bare-shouldered flamenco danseuses,
bulbous-bottomed hausfraus with their bloomers comically skewed,
globe-helmeted deep-sea divers with overspilling treasure chests,
a number of Iwo Jima flag-raisings, artichoke-derriered mermaids
and their trident-bearing paramours, guardian lions, borzois
(he *thinks* they're borzois: *some* kind of italicized dog), assorted
Viking warriors and strikingly-bonneted Indian chiefs
with feathered spears, and seemingly-endless frogs and mice and turtles
wearing human attire—snoods or zoot-suits or biker garb . . .
Okay then, pray for *my* people, he tells them.

My People

1: THE MYTHIC ADVENTURES OF LOUIE AND ROSIE

Shoyn Fergéssin: *"I've Forgotten"* in Yiddish

But now it's the Yiddish itself I'm forgetting;
it's back on the wharf, in a grimed-over jar
we can barely see into. What's this: is it a cameo brooch,
the bride's profile eaten-at by pickle-brine; or
is it a slice of radish? This is a tooth,
yes? We can turn that jar in the sun all day and
not be able to read it. There's a label, with a name
in black script dancing just beyond arm's reach.

———

A woman is weeping. What did he *do?* he asks
the noncommittal stars, the dark and rhythmic water,
even the slimy pilings. This is a wharf,
in summer. He tells her a joke, not that
it does much good. This is my grandfather,
Louie (in English). This is my grandmother, *Rosie.*
1912. They're in each other's arms again by morning
and don't need to say a word.

———

We'll find them, like ancient coins or arrowheads.
Now they can only be approximate. Here, washed up
on the beach: a few maxims, song titles, even that joke.
It goes: "'You're a Jew, how come you have a name
like Sean Ferguson?' He says, 'I was so frightened
when we landed at Ellis Island that I couldn't remember
anything for a minute. So that's what I said. They asked me
my name and I said *I've forgotten.'"*

1563

> ... the Northern masters painted as they did not from any lack
> of skill but from the insight that perceives that truth can
> sometimes be better conveyed by a pale, awkward figure than by
> a gloriously graceful one.
>
> Timothy Foote

1.

My grandmother's being ejected from the Mediterranean
sunniness, the seamless and unblemished scene, of a Titian painting.
I've tried to imagine her here, where sward as evenly unrolled
as a carpet leads to palace stairs; and gods, and courtiers
almost as perfect as gods, commingle. These are figures
whose bones are fashioned after Ionic columns, the women's hair is all
italic serifs, and their skin—there's lots of skin,
where robing coyly flounces open—is a peach-tone
alabastrine. So I thought she might enjoy the change, but:
"Voos iss doos?" she cries out, "What *is* this?"—she didn't

"take," a transplant that's refused. On the level of narrative,
she's dragged by palace bullyboys to the edge of the world and
roughly tossed away. On the level of medium, the tempera
spits her out like a seed. She falls through chilly
nowherespace, with only an infrequent ragged brushstroke,
like a shooting star, around her; then she lands
—in landscape, naturally. It's winter. Weather's a lash
on the back. Some bumpkin types, who look not unlike
lumpy burlap sacks of potatoes, are warming their butts
at a rubbish fire. 1563. At last!—my grandmother feels at home.

8

2.

The prestidigitory moon is levitating the oceanwaters
we've come to know as majestic, through their guest-appearance
in High Art: as the polyp-topped immensity of that tidal wave
of Hokusai's; or Turner's waters, smoothed by an iron of fog. Yes, but
no less is the bamboozling lunar magic on the fluids
of the body. In the creases of sex a boy has greasily crayoned
on a bathroom wall, the mysteries of Sky and Cycle,
Month and Menses, Human Flesh and the Heavens, are freighted
as richly as in a Titian nude (the egregiously relative talent
notwithstanding). At the same time Titian's statuesque and

shell-pink (sometimes sunset-gilded shell-pink)
lovers were being painted into those poses of classical scale,
symmetrical, graceful, something like geometry
moving pinkly through cream . . . beneath the snot-colored sky
of the endless Flemish winter, Bruegel painted people
as they are: their hands and faces are cracked hardpan,
some of them end in stumps at the knee, and every one of them
marked deeply by severity and compromise. Though lovers
must still dream each other raimented in glow. "Here—"
look, one hopeful fellow offers her his spot at the rubbish fire.

3.

There's a story my grandfather saved her from ruffians
under the pier, a small guy stirred by big love, vooming
circles through that fish air with a lead pipe, and the fear-shit
trickling out his hole. I don't know; if it didn't happen,
still, it's an accurate emblem of his 14-hour work days
in the truck bays of the packing plant, dirt pay
and a horse-ass foreman on the line. Each day he slew that dragon.
She had her heroics too: *you* try to raise three daughters
in a room above a pool hall, in Chicago, in sawdust, in 1912,
in Jewtown under the thunder of the el. But it could happen

in this Netherlandish city just that way, in this city
of armless beggars holding out their alms-cups in their teeth;
this city the sky grinds like a pestle; this city
of rats-in-the-crib; this city of faces chipped at,
by the passing days, like rough flint tools — and shook inside
the passing nights like dice the Devil games with. Even
here, though, the children are dancing: in and out
of a lopped hog's sputtering aorta. Even here, in sleep,
the psyche stomps in golden boots, enacting dramas
in shrewd clean lines: Timelessness, Rapture, Redemption.

4.

And she wasn't a möbius-strip-of-a-woman Miro
might have painted, she wasn't composed of any of Degas'
zygotic dabs, no, this was Grandma Rosie staring me down
to blushing in my 14th year—yes Grandma Rosie
knock-back-a-*schnapps*, oh Grandma Rosie plucker-of-guts,
a turnip-bodied galleon-breasted Bruegelian woman for sure,
in the shadow and half-light of the afternoon kitchen.
Here's what happened: I'd been spied. Some boozer busy
wringing out his dingus saw me, winked to the manager—there I was,
artiste of "dirty pictures" on the men's room tile, nabbed by them

red-handed (I mean the crayon was red) while working out the Beauty
and the Mystery of The Other in the only viable vehicle of expression I
    had
and here I was now, facing her, blamed and shamed and knowing
she knew how loathsome I was in the bottommost frogslime cell of my
    being.
What she did: she waited five full minutes, wholly silent minutes, awful
    ones;
then hugged me. No one painted that moment; she died a year later.
I've seen her since then in a Bruegel crowd scene, offering a pancake
to a terrified, blubbering child. He's a few quick strokes of wailing, and
she's . . . a tenderness, a breath of paint, a heft of peasant hipbones.

5.

A Bruegel crowd scene: you can count 500
Flemish men and women in one, and all of them
laying full claim to cheesy gums, and a greedy heart,
and a rattling-around nobility-bone the size of a knuckle,
and marrow that won't quit squeezing out the juice
of being human. Even toad-faced: human. Even wolf-grinned:
human. Even seeming to float in the air like a seraph: human.
I've seen it, I've heard its din, a great communal hubbuzz
rising into the gray of the Northern skies: *It's slough and renewal,*
slough and renewal, until the final skin.

Gallery

When my grandfather stepped from the boat
they gave him a choice of paintings to enter. "This one,"
he said by a nod of his head. Why not?—for weeks
in the bodystink quarters of steerage,
the lice had run as freely as milk through his crevices,
and the only food was saltbread softened in engine water,
but here, in *The Boating Party* by Renoir, it's spring,
the light is floral, even cloth and skin
are really petals in this light, the glass
the wine is in is alive in this light, the men are easy
in speaking with women (he noticed, oh especially,
the women), their mutual fascination is another flower
filling the air, and the clusters of fruits
looked as shining to him as an orchestra's brass section
—when he peeked around the corner of the painting, in fact,
he saw a grouse was simmering in peppered cream
and that settled it, he sat down at a nearby table,
listening to the bright and empty talk, his shy eyes
staring at his waiting plate. A server appeared
and left. On my grandfather's plate was a boiled potato,
only that. But he was starving, so he ate it. He ate it
indelicately, with an almost sexual fervor, and then
looked up to see the family around him,
with their corded hands, with their faces like worn-out shoes,
were eating theirs, just that, with a root tea. He
was in Van Gogh's *The Potato Eaters*. The room
was as dark as the tea. Outside, the wind was a punishing switch.
The talk was hushed and raw and familiar,
he was at home here, he was at home in the broken
light of the hanging oil lamp. When the meal was done,
he stepped out into the lane, he breathed the country dark in

hungrily, then walked. He needed a wife.
He needed a future. What did he see ahead,
when he squinted? He would barely understand
that man in Edward Hopper's *Nighthawks*,
on a distant corner, some depleted 3 A.M.,
was his son — who slides the dime for his java
over the counter, slants his hat, then heads out into streetlight
from the diner's unrelenting angles and planes.
He's lonely. It's 1942. He'd love to meet my mother,
someone humming a hot little tune
and pretty as a picture.

The Flowers of Koonwarra

The oldest known flower was discovered this past year, and it's not the stuff of poetry.

start of a science article

No. "A tannish gray fossil
about an inch long, it's not that
impressive." Nor would I write
about this lock of my grandmother's hair,
a feeble grab of strands
the color of soot and iron filings. She
may as well be 12 million years
gone. Why have her clumping home,
up the three peeling flights,
from a ten-hour day at the fish barrels,
sitting in shadow now, her shoes off,
rubbing her corns? And: *oy*,
she says to each of those painful blossoms, *oy*,
and *oy*, and "Nothing comes easy"
she mutters, *Gring kumpt keyn zach nit on*,
even her language is something we need
to chisel out from the heart of a rock.

In 1772 the British amateur chemist Joseph Priestly
showed that a plant and an animal, enclosed
inside an airtight chamber, created a system of gas exchange
that let both live — and so began the unprecedented
custom of flowers in sickrooms (which,
in those days, were normally shuttered against the air).
I remember: she had a dimestore vase on the sill,
green-gray, with crazing. How old was I, 15?
I remember they said the rest of us had to leave,

only Louie was left at her side, and 28 years later
I've discovered what to bring to her
small room in the earth: this fossil
from Koonwarra, Australia, to set on the ledge
in a version of that
last afternoon's chemical circuit.

———

She's brushing her hair, her lavish
wheatfield of hair. She's 16. Life
is as hard as an axe-handle, but
America and its double-shift at the fishworks
is impossibly far in the future and
today she's wearing her blouse with the roses
stitched around the rather daring neck,
and that's her name, Rose, so
this surely is a lucky blouse; today,
a lucky day. I can't retrieve much
more than this from the bombed-out cities,
the smog, the hundreds of little groin-fires,
solaces, petty scrambles, and layers of quicklime
in between: *Di tsayt ken alts ibermakhn,*
"Time alters everything." Yes. But I know Louie
is 16 too. And I can imagine him
mincing nervously up to the door—the speech
on fidelity practiced that morning, gone
all goosey and dumb on his lips,
but a rat-a-tat song of sex refusing to die
from some furry back cell in his brain.
He stares . . . She
sits there, calmly, in a ligament
of afternoon light that trembles and stretches
around her, and then he's
next to her, holding her, babbling, everything
fading away from my fancy of them except
for the bouquet I see
he's dropped, in his haste, in the doorway.

———

"Everything fading away . . . " I don't have but
one photo of them. I'm sending a book
about dinosaurs to my nephew Ian, their
greatgrandchild — those living armored mountains
in their scrupulous museum-wired otherness are
clearer to him than Louie and Rose could ever be.
They're on his t-shirt, his crayon case, his milk mug;
and their monstrousness is quaint to him, the way,
for instance, a war becomes
after the tv mini-series.

———

"Armored mountains" doesn't come close.
Crushers, slashers, every grain of surface turned
to brute adamancy. And even *Tetraceratops*,
the one we now believe was a link
on the way to mammals, is horned four ugly times
around its snout and once on either jaw,
with teeth like sharpened gate-posts.
It looks like simply touching one
in its sleep would draw blood from us, painful. And the mammals
that it *did* give rise to: painful. Things
all shield and fang.
Though surely they mated.
Surely they lay themselves
down in exactly these flowers.

A World Above Suffering

1.

When my grandfather Louie came here, from Chicago,
his phlegm was already marbled with blood.
So here he stayed for a year, in the flat
and unclogged light of the mountains,
and here he healed. He stayed on one year more,
a kind of payment, he helped with the gurneys and the pans,
in Denver, in 1906,
at the Jewish Sanitarium for Consumptives.

2.

Even near the giant windows, the air in the ward seemed brown
with institutional viscosity. Outside, though,
on the balconies designed to accommodate hospital beds,
the patients were lined up side-by-side like tiles in a game,
white tiles in sunlight.
                          In the left bed,
Morris Rosenfeld, the "sweatshop poet,"
"the voice of the people," coughing up the bunched threads
of his 15-hour days bent to the hemming machines or the irons
" . . . until I was a machine as well," he says, then starts
some quavering lines from one of his poems
of raw-throated grief and indictment.
                          In the bed on the right,
Yehoash (Solomon Bloomgarden), whom they called
"the Jewish Byron"—translator ("Hiawatha,"
even the Koran), lexicographer, diarist, and aspirant
to the gates of the lofty, "singingness" he termed it, and
he cultivated an Orientalist's interest

in the music of Chinese poetry, its willow and plum.

———

My grandfather tended to both of their enfeeblements,
the spit-cups and the soiled strips. In the afternoon light
of the balcony, which seemed to hit the three of them uninfluenced
by a single touch of the Earth, he'd listen bemusedly
to their conflicting Yiddish.

3.

Today they're reading new poems to each other.
"And this time, Mr. Shakespeares," says the nurse,
then wags her finger, "NO EXCITEMENTS! Louie,
see they shouldn't get heated." Last time, both of them
waxed apoplectic in righteous aesthetic wrath.
"Hokay now," Rosenfeld clears his throat
                                        and
we're back in an attic firetrap shirtwaist work pit,
tethered there by hunger to an 84-hour week, in the heat
that clambers on your naked shoulders pickaback,
in the piles of scrap and mouse-filth past your ankles,
in the insufficient gaslamp, eye wobble, wrist fatigue,
the stitch in the hem and its sister stitch
the razor-edged worm in your side. For this,
twelve dollars a week. For this, with twenty people breathing
thickly in a windowless room, the gaslamp trickling fumes,
the bucket toilet radiating waves of human waste in a corner.
Some of these workers are twelve years old, some in their seventies.
Rosenfeld soars in exhortation, then squinches his spirit down low
in hurt or self-pity, then takes off soaring
explosively again. "The time clock drags me off at dawn
to the corner of Pain and Anguish . . . "
                                    And Yehoash
is moved by this, and by the rocks and birds
his balconymate makes alternately with his gesturing hand.
It would be unfair, saying anything else; Yehoash
is moved, his eyes grow damply alive. But also

his work could be, as Irving Howe would later phrase it,
"willfully distant from any Jewish experience." This
afternoon, he reads lines modeled loosely on
"The Song of Picking Mulberry," "Song of Plucking Cassia,"
"A Fish Trapping Song," "The Cowherd's Song," and
"Song of the Woman Weaving," where, if there's complaint
(". . . the levy of the silk tax comes too early this year . . . "),
labor isn't pain so much
as cause for meditation, under the great, gong Chinese moon,
and weariness isn't more than mist
a white crane sculls obliquely through. He reads
about the Empress Yang-Tse-Fu, and in the Denver air
appear her hundred golden doors, her sapphire-sided palanquin
and honor guard. "And the cherry blossoms
settle on the shore," he ends.
                            So of course
in a moment they're squabbling, and their normally pale,
whey-blue faces ruddy the color of brick. "Boys!
BOYS!"—the nurse can see it from out on the lawn,
and yells up: "Louie, DO something!" And
my grandfather stands between them,
in their utterly befuddling adjacence, holding out
—ineffectually, for no particular reason
other than chance—a length of bandage gauze: something
like an ancient Egyptian attendant
whose mummies refuse to hold still.

4.

That night, my grandfather dreamed.
He was back in Chicago, following
the stink of the tenement twistways.
Here was the cart of herring piled like ingots,
just as he remembered: wavering
in their day's-end rank aurora . . . Here,
the rubbish mound to the height of a three-floor warehouse
with, as usual, some street kids sledding on greased planks
down its wormy length . . . Everything was real,

more than real. At one corner he saw a woman,
above, in a sixth-floor window, naked from the waist up.
It was an ironing sweatshop—the heat was too much.
Her breasts were small, but drooped with appalling weight
to the six floors of gravity. She was retching. "I don't CARE!
I need the air from the roof!"—then she disappeared from the window.
Now, in the dream, he saw her sitting at the roof-edge
as the rim of the city turned the burning tulip colors of sunset.
It was cooler here; her breast-flesh pebbled slightly in the air.
The moon came out, the whole of a wheel-of-cheddar moon. She
started singing, it was "The Song of the Hemmer and Ironer":
Near dawn the pigeons stitch the sidewalks.
Later, at noon, the streets of my city are ironed
By the August sun.
Mother, a life is harsh but also beautiful.
Father, the rhythm of the piecework is a red thread
In my wrist. At night I want to unfasten this immense
Bone button in the sky, and see what's on
The other side of the night, if work is required there too.
Let the ladies of the court play their flutes
And peek at the day from behind their fans.
I'm going down into the streets, I'm going
To dance stitch-stitch in the gutters!

———

Then he woke. "China,"
he thought—and he would always picture this roof—
"a world above suffering."

———

He woke, he washed, he walked into another shift
of pads and ointments. Everything
was ahead of him still. He, who believed so much
was behind already, in merely his getting here . . .
everything was ahead of him still. The caged-up days
in the elevator, wearing the liver-colored-and-gold-braid
organ grinder's monkey outfit, whisking the buyers
of silk kimonos and homburgs to their appropriate floors . . .
the fish store, and the failure of the fish store, and

20

the dented awl for chipping the pike from its jacketing ice . . .
and Rosie, meeting Rosie, wooing Rosie in the candle-lit dinge,
and sticking with Rosie, over whatever
decades of sexual ardor, scrimping, and piety made their life then . . .
all of it waited for him, in him, was a seed
inside my grandfather as he lathered his hands, then
wheeled his charges into the immediate sun.
Both Rosenfeld and Yehoash would be cured, and off
to their individual destinies. But that would be long after
Louie packed his satchel and took the train away
from the mountain of poems and wetly rumbling lungs.
Enough was enough.

5.

Years later, back in Chicago now, he wandered
into Chinatown. Not the tourist version; the actual
squat-in-a-corner thing. He recognized
the ghetto poverty, the open ghetto
furnace of a heart—although the milky smoke
unwinding from the joss sticks wasn't his,
nor the amazing hothouse orchid-like fish
in pails on the peddler carts. A man named Lee Hsün
stopped him, he was so obviously lost.
"Fella, where you from?" He meant
what neighborhood, but my grandfather answered
"From Poland."
                    "Ah—Poland!" And Lee's eyes
widen in admiration.
"Poland! Princesses! Palaces!"

The Story of Dorsett

It's 1912. A man, or really a youth—he's just 18—
is loosely following the tracks of the Northern Comet
down a mild grade to where, at the infinity point,
the rails touch as daintily as mantis-paws
—and beyond even that, is the city. It might take him two,
three days on foot. If he were white
he'd ride the train, but that's not what he's bitching about.
My name is Dorsett Talman, my pappy's po' but freeeee.
My woman gots legs thatll make a man beg
And she ran away from me. I tell you she ran away from me.
He has a banjo as broke and repaired as a prizefighter's beak,
and sixty-four cents. And he has a name written down,
The Hi-Step Cabaret, where Lottie Mae is singing gospely jazz
for white folks every night, they call her Coffee Browne.

If only they were two countries but they're
a man and a woman. If only they were two planets
but they're a man and a woman. If only
they were positive and negative subatomic jots of emptiness
in outer space, they might align
according to a likelihood of opposites aligning
on the level of light and below light, but
they're a man and a woman, hopeless, floating,
goodbye. I *said* "goodbye." I don't care
what you said, I'm not about to leave. Look, maybe we
could talk this over. Would you like a drink? Your people drink
a lot. *My* people? Now wait a goddam minute, buster,
etc. If only scales, and fur. If only motion, and absolute zero.

22

I went me down to the river, its water was mocha-brown,
Its sides sudsed up like a shaving mug. And Lord I wanted to drown.
Up on the banks of the river, where the grasses are soft as beds,
A boy was going over his lover's body for chiggerheads.
Each one he found in her sweet sweet skin, he burnt it out with a match.
Dorsett is one of the lucky ones: can read a little, write a little,
can strike with his tongue like lightning when he makes a song
For every one she kissed him—Lord, that fever easy to catch!
I used to know that mocha girl, I used to be that boy,
But one fine night she took to flight . . . he stops
at a stand of loblolly pine, considering a rhyme word . . .
Oy-oy-oy-oy-oy-oy, my grandfather sings, stepping out of the greenness.
He's just a few days off the boat, he still has the stench
of a shack in Poland hovering over the folds in his clothes.

———

I mean the stink of parasitic goat and damaged cabbage,
I mean the miserystink a neighborlady named Dzidka left him,
fuming off the skin of his heart like a teakettle burn. So
they have a language in common, these two. Louie
thinks the *schwartzerman* is as black as the devil he saw once
snapping pigs' necks in a picture book—but he could use a little
of the devil on his side, in this befuddling country. Dorsett
has a use for Louie, too: they don't let niggerboys
pass notes through nightclub side doors, he knows *that.*
If this were a movie . . . but this is a paste-and-sawdust
homage to the sonnet. If this were a movie we'd follow
the hesitant ups and downs of their buddydom,
over the haze-skirted hills, with background banjo music
segueing into a throatily honkytonk big city sax.

———

And then even the cockbone moaning of the sax is only a ghost
in the air, the audience applause is like a grease stain on the darkness
of the empty club, the manager's saliva is evaporated
off her neck: and the woman the signboard barkers out to the world
as *Our Most Moving Cocoa Chanteuse* kicks her jillion-dollar heels off
and sits alone at 4 A.M. at a first-row table, reminding herself
that for all of the clawing and tawdriness around this game, there
is a glory in pouring forth her songs in front of the customers like
the only tigerlily on a dull lawn; anyway what else
was there back home?—peas to shell and ticks on her ass. Here,
it's limos and French liqueurs, and she can pretend this
Polack scrub-girl doing the floor (she's not alone by just that
much) is her personal servant. A pale slip of a thing. They
giggle together sometimes. My little *tadPole*, Lottie Mae jokes.

———

Say it's 1912. You're at a wintered-over river waiting
heart-in-mouth for Houdini to surface with unchained wrists.
You're one of a crowd: the stogie-chomping goofus
on your right, the bonneted fräulein on your left, and dozens
others, it could be a hundred. What does it mean, that you're become
this negligible asterisk in The Story of Houdini, like a figure
lost in landscape in an ancient Chinese scroll? Of course
the people assembled puffing out their white breaths here are
asterisks in The Story of You—that raggedy Jew and his
colored compadre, stomping their feet on the far bank, for example—
but it isn't the same. Do we ever know who
the "protagonist" is? Does anyone care the nation-states
of Europe are whetting their edges for war? The fräulein flourishes
off her bonnet, and look: it's Houdini! Everyone roars.

———

I keep calling him my grandfather but he won't be
that for 36 years—it isn't even a glimmer now, it's
farther than rockets or television. All he is
is a man in an alley, holding a note his friend wrote
in his fist, he's scared a copper is likely to thrash him
before its delivery. And the friend?—this is The Story of Dorsett,
yes, but as it's come to me through mishmashed half-facts,
genre-tainted clichés, and wildly-shuffled timeframes
of my family's gossipy sense of its history. Dorsett,
I'm sorry, is starting to melt. Now he's gone. It's only
Louie, cold and confused, with newspaper in his shoes.
He doesn't know the small magic that's going to happen. It's
4 A.M. He mumbles one more *oy*, then knocks. The woman
who's going to be my grandmother opens the club's side door.

The Jewish Poets of Arabic Spain
(10th to 13th Centuries),
with Chinese Poets Piping Out of Clouds
(and Once an Irishman)

1.   *A brother or a sister poet is constantly over our shoulders.*

                                                      Sosho

Gone, the last of the copcar sirens.
Gone, the final whine of a neighbor's midnight lust
for powertrimming his frowzy hedge.

                          ———

I'm watching you sleeping.
Your lids have set down
their harps.
I'm watching the breath-flesh rise and fall;
                                        and
Judah ha-Levi is writing
There is no likeness unto your beauty,
The apple's shape is your breast's shape, oh
The apple's hue is your cheek's hue.
                          I'm thinking
about the wall a disagreement raises
even between two people who love; and even with bricks
the size of grains of dust, it keeps
their separate sides of the bed
inviolate;
            and
Judah ha-Levi is writing
My love could wash her clothes
In the pour of my tears. My eyes are hers
For well-water.

                    I'm leaving
the bed, I'm staring—not the first time, either—
blankly out the window, at the siamese-twin blankness
of the night, attached by where my forehead
leans against the window pane; a night
like this, and Tu Fu wrote
I'm empty, here at the edge of the sky
—what Ku-t'ai-ch'ing called *idle grief*.
For hours, I'm a thinnest balance
walking the long insomnia-lines
of my own face, holding discourse
with the mirror, for everyone, asking it
those grayish questions of want and likelihood,
act and intent . . . the brief bare glances inside of ourselves
that the day won't allow
and the dark is ashamed of.
                            And these are the words
of Judah ha-Levi's I take back
to the pillow with me:
                    How shall I go through the narrow straits?
He may as well be writing it
in this room, it may as well be the 11th century, anytime
sleepless, any century full of moons like dinner plates,
and any language, and any people:
How shall I go through the narrow straits?

                    ————

And Wang Shih-chen (about 1700):
Now there's someone rapt in meditation;
It's midnight and still he hasn't gone to sleep.

27

2.

. . . phosphenes, the scientific word for the "stars" you see
when your head gets banged and for the scenes that appear
when you're half-asleep or when you meditate with your eyes
closed. Between the ages of two and four, when a child can
hold a crayon but knows little of how to draw objectively, he
is most apt to draw things with a distinctly phosphene char-
acter. And this is about equally true of primitive humans who
lived during mankind's childhood, to judge by the phosphene-
like figures in some of the prehistoric cave paintings . . .

arranged from Guy Murchie

Is this the story of Cain and Abel? It
could be, it's that early: this is another green day
(before the idea of "days") on a planet of scavengers and gatherers
at the cusp of learning hunting. Let's say . . . oh,
two million years ago, by potassium-argon dating. A man
—an almost-man—awakes in the unslaked chill of dawn,
beside his almost-woman. His face is bleeding, so
is hers, but they're alive: more than the strange-one is,
on the other side of the glade. *His* skull is crushed, and we
can match that indentation to the responsible
—to the specific responsible—antelope leg bone.
Here it is, in the hand of our near-man. Pain
is a flickering diadem in his head; he
closes his eyes,
              the Ice Age cave walls, figurines, and wands,
scored-over with their star/wave/crisscross sacred doodles,
go by in a dream;

when he opens his eyes it's 192 A.D.
Wang Ts'an is writing:
One goes to war when the lord commands,
Such decrees cannot be disobeyed.
This frontier post brings nothing but sorrow,
On the road there are starving women,
White bones cover the plain.
And yet he still might lift his head from his paper and hum
a traditional melody:
Tenderly I think of my lovely one,
Clouds fly, I cannot forget her.
                    So. There
is always the war. There has never not
been the war. It's simply more or less
legitimized at times. And
there is always this couple
at 4 in the morning, in bed, their asses touching
but their heads in different worlds.
Outside, the rumble then thunk of the garbage truck.
It wakes me for a moment
from my single hour's sleep, and through such milky
pinhole consciousness, the universe
floods in: its stars /
its waves / its encompassing crisscross.

————

Then I doze back into my half of the pattern
a diner waitress would call out to the cook
(two-over-easy-on-toast)
as "Adam and Eve on a raft."

3.   *Az men dermont zikh on dem toyt iz men nit zikher mitn lebn.*
            (If you start thinking about death, you're no longer
            certain about life.)

Yiddish proverb

All afternoon we watched the American bombs
and the Iraqi bombs, and counted the bodies; and, even so,
the television distances this suffering:
its final effect is about the size of a cigarette burn
inside us . . . No wonder
we quarrel that night:
                    to hurt, to remember
we *can* be hurt. That's
part of it anyway—who could ever wholly understand
the vendettas of intimate partners?
No wonder so often we let ourselves be lost
in some interior fog . . .

. . . it thickens
near the river. When he pushes off from shore
it's thicker yet, and soon it holds
his barely-room-for-two excursion-boat completely,
which is what he wants: to float there
for a while like a dull thought, in a mind erased.
Now he dah-dah-dahs under his breath. And now
he tries out some lines of a burgeoning poem,
"Flowers and grass appear far and hazy,
A crested loon flies into the current—
I ask myself what kind of man am I." Then:
"*Yah, yah,* I know jost vot you mean," a voice says in a Yiddish-inflected
Arabic. Well, Li Po startles: he thought he was alone in this mist but
no, he has a passenger barely visible beside him, who says:
"There is nothing for me in the world but the hour in which I am.
It lasts but a moment, and, like a cloud, is no more."
And Samuel ha-Nagid leans back, pleased with his phrasing.
Li Po is excited, he nearly drops the oar—now *this* is someone
he can talk to! "The river flows east,
And the gibbons cry. Men die in the wilds,

30

Vultures feed on human guts.
Sideways I look westward and I heave a long sigh."
Yes! Yes! His passenger nods in agreement!
"Man runs toward the grave,
And rivers hasten to the great deep.
I look up to the sky and its stars,
I look down to the earth and its creeping things.
The days of my sorrow are not complete."
A willow-dabbled bend in the water is going to deliver them
out of view, and Li Po is about to go breathily on
about cranes, or bamboo, or flowering plum, when: "Wait!
Wait!"—I'm running along the riverbank, pacing them.
"What about looooove?" I shout. They turn to me
with a look on their faces that says I've asked them something
so impossible it's even beyond
the speck-by-speck reflection
of *their* lotus-and-shtetl philosophy.

4.   *It is tempting to conjecture how much love poetry was ever written by the Hebrews, and is now lost to us forever, because it was not regarded as Holy Writ.*

David Goldstein

She: As the two scrolled sides of the *Torah* roll apart
    To reveal the scripture of the day,
    So you roll me apart to reveal the text of the night,
    My love, my lion-of-the-desert, my blossom.

And the stewardess is demonstrating the oxygen mask in America.
And the hotel elevator has no 13th floor in America.
And the mint is under the pillow of the freshened bed in America
And in Paris, which is America, and in Rome, which is America,
O and any day now in Zimbabwe. Come beneath the sheets
With me, Room Service will bring us a light California wine.

He: I went to see the flocks, and they were shapely on the hill,
    But not so shapely as you, to me, my gazelle, my oasis.
    I went to the orchard, and it opened up its sweetness for me,
    But yours is supreme, but yours is the privilege,
    My dove-of-the-towers, my almond.

"Pisa pallor," they said to our America ears, in Tokyo,
Which is America. There, in the pizza parlor,
Ravenous boys check out the ravenous girls, and also the other
Way around. There is no stopping American blue jeans or the wanting
Of what fills them to exquisitude, in Stockholm, or Lima,
Or Dzubovich, or on MTV, which is America, darlin'.

Both: The wrath of Adonai is great:
    The flood, and the dust, and the locust.
    But the season changes; the clemency of the seasons never dies,
    It will last through even the tempest, even the fire.
    Last night we were a storm,
    We were a cloud as hard as a shield,
    Its light was flung spears.
    Let us wake into a newer weather,
    My bulwark, my ewe at the delicate shoots,
    My flame kept lit in the Temple.

And the genders are revving their engines, automotive and sexual
Equally, and cruising the downtown drags of our America, and love
Is being made on Bible School retreats, on toxic dumps, and love
Is in that hidden island tribe that just a year ago was Neolithic and
Now of course is America, boomboom music and Coke and freedom
And escrow and give me a kiss in the high school halls,
In the shopping malls, in the golden skyscraper walls
O of America.

Yüang-yang, mandarin ducks, are Chinese symbols
of "conjugal happiness." Chiang Ch'un-lin sees
Thirty-six pairs in a lovely pattern,
Together they bathe in the clear brook.
And for Yeats? "The Wild Swans at Coole"
" . . . paddle in the cold / Companionable streams or climb the air"
(how?) "lover by lover." It's 1917.
Or is it 810? Yüan Chen is writing
As I sit watching the morning sun come up,
A flock of birds returns by twos.

5.   *Returned from dream, I rested for a while*
            and wept profuse tears . . .

Huang Tsun-hsien

Then waking: rubbing another marquee
of phosphenes out of my eyes.

———

Beside me, you're first lazily breaking
out of the gluey webbing of sleep.
And over us . . .
                    something . . .
                            maybe the future
is here in the room above us,
is looking in for a minute—fondly?
could I think it's fondly?—not unlike the way
I'm remembering back to those lines of Samuel ha-Nagid's:
    Come out and see the morning light
    —A scarlet thread in the East!

———

I think it's the future. At least, it's the future
we called "tomorrow." Here it is,
"today": one hundred cups of effort,
good intentions, small misunderstandings,
stretching away from the bed
and finally leading back to it.

———

Who are they, anyway?—watching us
staring each other, watching us willing
the first emotional patch
sewn over our last emotional wounding.
I think we do it for them. The future always needs
the wistful story of disrepair and mending
to play out its pain in a handful of verses,
to heal itself in a handful more.

———

Sometimes the first of me given over
unto another day has been the skin
raised by the touch of your tongue
— the first, and the best,
of the compromisings
of self in a welter of others.

———

The traffic jam and the headlines are waiting.
Come, my pomegranate, my swan.
The memos and sirens and deals are waiting.
Come, my candle, my crown, my song.

———

Headlong into it — each of us is both
the herder *and* the herd.
As if just to drive our own shadows before us,
to market, is labor enough.

My People

2: MARRIAGE IN TRANSLATION

The Books / P, L, E

The usual troubles stumble in, in the usual morning light.
She's still asleep. He snugs his ear against her skull,
as if to eavesdrop on her version of things, but it's all like noise
he might hear with a glass held to the wall
of some adjoining motel room: tantalizing; vague. By now the light
makes clear the little altars of Money and Love we call
a day, so now he's up, and now he's buttoned up, and now
he's ready to head toward the upkeep of both of those
ever-eroding structures. He sees Billy's awake, already lost
in another one of those mystery-series-for-kids page-turners:
Little did the twin sleuths suspect it, but soon this innocent
thimble would plunge them headlong into The Mystery of
The Outer Space Invaders! But in the Book of the Grownups,
a man and a woman each remembers buying new coffee and
yet the tin's half empty. They had the agency send a plasterer
over and someone with sacks of dirt called "fill," but still
the cellar oozes. "He was called Phil?" "*What?*" There are Mysteries
and mysteries, he thinks; and if a UFO did glitter down some slant
     of light
as solid as a playground slide, it's no more amazing than that
sun reaches Earth at all, and holds this cup, this saucer.

Arnie and Marnie Baumgartner are The Baumgartner Twins
from "The Baumgartner Twins and the Rodeo Desperado,"
"The Baumgartner Twins and the Digital Werewolf," etc. Hip
kids, hip adventures. When they look in the mirror and you look
with them, *as* them, you see someone laboring hard
through this world to do good. Time and again, their chance for this
is on the level of saving rajahs' thrones from hooligans and
foiling counterfeiters. This time, Grandpa Tequila-Schotz
the Secret Service Op is vacationing with The Twins in an Africa
still untouched by the ofay 20th century, when a runner bears
an emergency message coded as stains on an ivory thimble:
a UFO is reported landed on Mt. D'dend—will
Grandpa Tequila-Schotz safari there ahead of various nefarious
foreign spies who are also zeroing-in on the alien spacecraft? Hooboy, will
he! He tells Mel One-Eye the porter to ready the jeep, but Billy's
no fool and by the way Mel pouts and slouches we can see
he's up to "no good." Meanwhile, some animal lets out a roar
the size of a toolshed. His mother calls him down to cornflakes.
At the tip of a dark-fronded palm, some luxurious African flower
sways and waves like the Rose Queen assuming her float.

———

But in the Book of the Grownups it isn't, it's never, that
clear. First, over breakfast she discovers Billy heisted
the handful of coffee—some attempt to stain one of her milk glass
curio thimbles, "for an adventure" is all he'll say, then her
punitive ire, then his tears and *"I hate you!"* That night
she stares in the bathroom mirror as if at a lab test specimen.
The son she loves hates her. And later, she dreams: a woman
is shipwrecked, alone for years on an island. One day
walking the rind of beach, she finds a board washed up,
with the letters P, L, E stenciled on it, obviously
broken from out of a larger construction, a word. PLEASE?
APPLES? This becomes the central, impassioned
mystery of the woman's life—some word, at last, from
Out There, that she needs to solve, a test, a sign . . . She
wakes with SPLEEN and PLEASURE floating her mind.
The man she loves is asleep. The blocky, male weight of him,
as ever, repels and consoles. And he must see her
too as a fragment of something familiar, some shard
from a vastly comforting native language he can't quite
comprehend. She strokes him. PLEXUS? NIPPLES?

The PLEIADES goes down. At lunch in the company cafeteria he
sees a grainy helicopter camcorder shot of a child's squeezetoy
space ship slipping pathetically through the gray Atlantic chop. A plank
with part of the liner's name in stencil bobbles by, a woman's straw hat . . .
It makes him want to drop updating Accounts Received and
speed through 14 miles of noon-rush red light snarl
to hold them both, to hold them into some critical human tightness
where forgiveness forms, and whatever safety there is in numbers
counts. He doesn't, of course. The Book of the Grownups has no space
for that, and he returns to his ledger. Billy returns
to his megamillion-thrills African hijinks, but it doesn't
quite provide its usual spell; he's seen the same noon news show
over his baloney-and-banana snack, and all day the ghost
of that missing child, a ghost composed of TV snow
and oceanwater, follows him disconsolately about the house
and over the lion-filled veldt to Mt. D'dend. Not
that, in any case, things look so great for our heroes: Marnie
has just discovered a leak in the gas tank. Yes, and though
she's plugged it with that thimble, spirits glumly dip. "Someone,"
says Tequila-Schotz suspiciously, "is up to no good!"

———

This is what he knows: his child, the boy-one, B'ahlee,
is curled in the hut, all-day-many-days, with the blue worm
sickness. This they can cure, in the medical compound
seven-waters away, but it takes "gimme" as it's called here,
money: already he's worked an extra field this season, worked
all night until the moonedge dissolved like a mineral powder
in dawn, and still it isn't enough; and the gimme-gourd rattles
most piteously; and the boy-one coughs up thin
swamp-color phlegm; and his own belovéd, Bride-Price-7-Cows
the yamroot of his heart, every morning looks at the pictures
in magazines of houses with a car in front and sighs those
hurtful, rich miasmal sighs she's perfected, and this
can also be cured one way or another, but each way
requires the same. The truth is, these white-ones are aliens
to him as surely as if they'd landed from Alpha Centauri
and marched down a gangplank of protons and fizz. And so,
for a fee, he's punctured their gas tank—so? He squints
his one eye and stares in the pond's calm surface. It's
his book; and the sky, and the tree-bark. He squints and
he sees an innately good person squint back.

———

"Go left." "Right." "No, left." "That's right: left."
"So?" "What?" "Sew what?" Etc. The I-to-Thou-and-back
Translation Dictionary has yet to find its Webster; meanwhile,
the dark, the almost varnish-dark, oils of Flemish interior scenes
define our own insides, and whatever scant candle-length love brings
looking for clarity: stutters, beats against the dark and fails,
repeating little flickers of its insufficient light. She wakes and
sees him at the bureau weeping over her old straw hat. It's
sweetly poignant somehow, and yet creepy; when he recovers
and stumbles to bed, the utter strangeness of it quickens in her,
meeting, as an equal, the level of his ferocious
/ when was the last time he wanted her this way?/ need for flesh
on flesh, and it deepens their lovemaking. Later,
she studies him sleeping—knee-jut at an angle, and the hands
in a sloppy knot, just like Billy. Somewhere hundreds of miles
inside him, their hour of sexual meshing-together means
—what? She wants to see his dreaming's by-products
rising, moon slivers, beast feces, blood flowers, pussies,
fetal twins, eel shapes, human wings, anything . . . diacritical marks
by which she might start to pronounce his language.

———

The good ship SPLENDID JOURNEY sank and was combo-atomic
transport-rayed by Scientists from Another Planet, for study,
to the topmost snowy crags of Mt. D'dend—thus say two sailors who
survived the original wreck and the prodding by alien doctors
("They had us stick our tongues out and say *ahhh*—it must be
universal," Taylor the sailor observes) and so are pleased
to be rescued by Arnie and Marnie Baumgartner and the dotty,
resourceful Tequila-Schotz. The spies and fang-crammed
jungle beasts have all been overcome—for now, it's
hot chocolate brewed on the wheezing jeep's radiator, some jokes,
and a well-earned sleep. *The twin sleuths couldn't guess it but
soon this radiator cap would be the clue that solved their
next adventure, the Mystery of/* he closes the book. He
hears them through his bedroom wall: the shudder-and-thump
he's learned from friends is "fucking," which became the name
he's given to a make-believe planet: Fucking, someplace
farther away than he can imagine being. If it's scary, it's
familiar fright—he's heard their love before—and it replaces
the drowned boy's ghost. He starts to drowse now, while
this page from the Book of the Grownups flutters back and forth.

———

Lapwings have "vibration feathers"; diving, these
produce a special courtship thrum—to think of this
can scramble one's marrow in wonder. But for us, each day
that takes us further into the Book of Us is only a few more
worrisome dollars, a couple of drunken kisses, a fist,
some plans for ruling the world, a flat tire. It's night.
Then the water's decorated with scatterings of orange light
like a jumbled-up skeleton waiting for resurrection: and
yes, in a while the sun does fully rise. Another day
of ourselves, as "ourselves" in "Another Day of Ourselves."
It's so easy to see them this morning: a woman, a man,
the child they love they raise and fret through. It's
so wholly possible to imagine their glee and their fracas,
to nail them up for a mirror, as they peer in
their mirrors, adjusting the finelined interweave
of consciousness. Now Billy returns the lousy little thimble.
It's so easy to love them, or feel the spit go slowly sour over them,
then to file them away. Now dawn is nearly here,
one broomstraw of its lumens floats the murk out my window . . .
I'm stamping their notebook COMPLETE.

Thermodynamics / Sumer

Heave-and-buckle, the furnace warbles its heat up
out the naked livingroom window. The new house
shrinks and its occupants shiver: we need drapes.
Not now, this isn't time for anything
thinking accomplishes. You say you saw your sister
leave her grave that way—a wavery and elemental rising

up the dug shaft, and then skyward, as if heaven
and our long approach were a matter of schoolbook
thermodynamics. Maybe. What I know is, your face,
pale at the graveside, turned to clear glass you
half left through—following her out of love,
I imagine—and all week you haven't completely

returned. In this—in death, that is—as in so much
of life, the ancient peoples did it to a literal completion
our subconscious dramas symbolize. Beneath two quilts
and a blanket, I'm reading about the Sumerian
burial pits that Woolley discovered: always,
the royal personage in a stone room, then

the sloping ramp leading down to it, filled
with the bodies of men of the royal guard
and ladies-in-waiting—67, in one case—each
with the small metal cup for the poison alongside,
all of them having ritually lain themselves in ordered rows
while the harpist provided theophany music

until her nimble fingers also woozied, cooled, and fell.
It's something I would share with you tonight but you're
all shell; and if part of you isn't, it's somewhere
beyond our describable planet of physical objects
and simple needs. For the length of the stay, for some while at least,
I'll be losing your warmth to that other world.

16th Century, Brush and Ink:
A Hermit on a Riverbank

is virtually *all* riverbank: the water is a great
and lazy wash across the picture plane,
as smooth as unrolled silk—in fact
its one disturbance, way at the right,
where two rocks make for choppiness, is
as decorative as the tassel-pull on a scroll.
The brush has done the water drier
in the distance, so there's no firm line
where sky begins, there's only the feeling
of foggily being led to such a vastness,
even the mountains are dwindled to milkteeth
and the mighty pines of the north to a raggedy
line. Oh, and the hermit?—*so* small: an asterisk
to a footnote that barely serves to remind us

people exist at all. He's like a mote,
a fleck of grit, caught in the rhythm of the planet's
breathing. The serenity I think
I see surrounding him—a calm
the pinpoint stippling seems to mean—may
be a function of this obvious unstature. *He*
hasn't argued all night with the woman he cares for,
over some this-or-that of angst they rolled up
from spittle and dust. No, he's just doing splish-splash semi-zen,
lounging-around near the shallows, and telling me,
"Boobeleh, give an ear: reduce yourself. Your
cockamamie books and froufrou, even this poster
of *me*—*ffft*, into the trash! I'm talking pride and ego,
boychik. Go, we sages say, with the flow." But

what he doesn't know—*can't* know—that I know
effortlessly, is that the man who's inked him here
in what one art professor's called "this very
rivery reverie" will be dead in a year, his eyes
gouged out by a special device intended for that
efficient use alone, his brush-hand sawed off
at the wrist by a common dull gardening knife.
The Emperor's men will do this for a fee and
the Emperor order it done for a Cause. I imagine
"Justice" or "Equality" is how we'd say its ideogram.
"The Truth" is always a good one. And the truth is,
concepts dwarf us as surely as landscape. We're
mere grains of silt, against anything
ending in -ology or -ism. Rabbi Guru-san,

I'm sorry, m'man: today I'm saving this
repro of you from the rubbish, today I'm glorying in
each kitschy souvenir toothpick holder and sno-globe
wearing its sumptuous lei of fingerprints that say
I'm around on this planet. I'm not ready for letting
these proofs-of-me drift into an oblivion thermal,
lose themselves in History or the Infinite, and wink out
with the rest of the sputtering embers up there in the night,
no. You can work at meditating yourself outside
of your own sweet skin, you have my blessing; but today
I'm making peace with this woman and reaffirming our
armful of personal flesh. You know how *huge* the universe is?
—Sometimes we'll hurt each other just to remember
we haven't been dissolved into it yet.

Would you know a Snook, or a
Large-eyed Whiff, from a Goggle-eyed Scad,
should the necessity arise? . . . I thought so.

Will Cuppy

Add it to the list. Add *moazagotl*,
"one or more cloud banks formed on the lee side
of a mountain under foehn conditions." *Say wha'?*
What we don't know, fills — overspills — our days
so copiously it's our major response and,
therefore, likely our major mode of journeying
through that mysterious thing "the human condition"
— though just now I'm in a plane, and passing
over a dove-brown checkered terrain
that's obviously . . . *something*, moor or loess,

topography being a subject as certainly hidden-away
from my feeble powers of understanding as, say,
whatever graceful orrery glints and swivels
in the stewardess's skull: small joys? swift pain?
the dumb blitz of the sleep-deprived? — I don't know,
but suspect it bears no speck of similarity
to this successfully flirtatious scenario squirting
through my noggin. Remember those baked clay spheres
the ancient Sumerians sent their messages in, that needed
cracking open? — that's one human head to another. Travel

intensifies, or at least reminds us intensely of,
this. I'm flying home to my wife with a carry-on bag
of some standard Goldbarthian booty — three
bright 1950s dimestore toy tin outerspace ray guns
swaddled inside three equally-antique outerspacegirl-patterned

boxer shorts—and she'll meet me at the airport with
a touch of our by-now complacent sexual ease in the air;
she'll obligingly *ooh* as I unwrap these three trophies with
a Barnum-like spiel; then we'll shnoogle, and tumble
tangled to sleep with our craniums inches away and our dreams,

like everyone else's, so impossibly foreign it might take real
rocketships light-years to gravitate down. George Borrow,
traveling Spain in 1835, reports "a burly savage-looking
fellow" and his femme companion "as savage as himself," both
Catalans, and "under the influence of an incomprehensible
fury." These two argue, then he draws a knife, and stabs
at her bosom; "however, she interposed the palm of her hand,
which was much cut." With that and a curse, he leaves, and
Borrow rushes up to the trickling woman, offering British flurries
of concern for her well-being. "She

turned her countenance upon me with a sneer: 'Cannot
a gentleman be conversing with his lady upon their own
private affairs without being interrupted by *you?*'" So
much is beyond Berlitz. While Boston didn't seem to mind,
in Kansas City I looked up from the security x-ray rollerbelt
into the itchy professional scowls of four armed guards, while one
by one my ray guns were gingerly undone from their shorts
and held aloft for the edification of two Detective Lieutenants and
what had turned by this time into a sizeable crowd
—the toys' shapes having, of course, been translated wholly

opaquely onto the screen as serious weaponry. Even
that famous (and I think spectrally lovely) world's first
x-ray Röntgen chanced on . . . Didn't I read it's
the janitor who's one-layer-deeper-than-nakedly exposed
here, bone geometry flensed of all secrets?—and
his rings of keys at his hip with my ray guns' opacity, his
jingling catch of tiny saw-toothed snook and whiff and scad. What
daily privacies do they open for him? We don't know, let it
stand for what we don't know, what's locked
darkly from us under foehn, or any, conditions.

How Easy It Is

A family is murdered: husband, wife,
a 5- and 6-year-old. The bolt is sawed off
cleanly, and the slits in the throats
are neat professional slits,
as if four envelopes were opened: even the signature
the killer left, a scoring on the cheek of each,
is neatly figured, bingo- or tictactoe-like.
The town is horrified. Although these deaths
are dust motes in the dunes of death
that pile and reshape themselves and could cover a city
daily—still, the town in which these four
were slaughtered is horrified, and that night
wives and husbands surreptitiously eye
the common comings and goings of their own homes
with emotions that surpasseth understanding.
There are few clues. Days go by. A man
admits to having nightmares, and is sure
he committed the murders while in a trance,
and shows up weeping at the station. A woman
phones, all week she hasn't been able to bring herself
to lift the kitchen knife to simply dice a carrot,
even her emery file makes her skin crawl: she did it,
she knows she did it, sleepwalking, hypnotized,
let them come and drag her to a cell.
The detective assigned to the case wakes up
that day, and dons his good detectiveware, and
kisses his wife and son on their cheeks,
and drives to an office he finds is swimming
in various written, phoned, and in-person confessions.
They come from every neighboring state. It seems
that half the planet realizes how easy it is

to damage a family. There are hundreds of confessions
and not one real suspect. Maybe the local
cops aren't doing a good enough job. A pressure
fills the squad room. There are forms, and reporters,
and more forms, and a nasty call from the mayor,
and by day's end our detective is a tightening engine
of knots being powered by coffee. How did it
go, his wife asks; GODDAMMIT, he says,
in front of the son,
in the loudest voice he's used in their own
six years together. She brings her hands up
to the sides of her face, as if he's actually hurt her there.

Will the Real Shakespeare Please Stand Up?

The bar is called *The Duck Blind* and is decorated with decoys
—of which, antique models are highly prized: the verisimilitude
daubwork on those compact backs, etc., and the cartoonier
ones as well. A man in a back booth is saying
he's tight pals with the tv producer community—would she
like to pose for a promo portfolio, over at his apartment?
Oh he's good, he's smooth as dental floss—but
lying, through those perfect pearly teeth. In fact he wants
to use the knife on her, like on the others, an inch
at a time, the face first, till they plead. And she's all

golly whiz, wow *would* she! as she nervously swizzles sloe gin.
She's a cop. Her "Nude-Lift Casbah Bra" is
wired for sound, and three guys monitor her in a van that
says (cop humor here) MAMMA REE'S STEREO SERVICE.
"Let's go then—ready?" The "beef-katoothpick" "snax"
they've rearranged ten dozen ways on their plates without eating
are gravy-dyed soy substitute, and from this screen
at the side of the bar, the President is mouthing like a carp
—if we could hear him, he'd be promising us he did or he didn't,
whichever we care to choose. And so my theme is deceit,

its intricate, dolorous beauty. William Henry Ireland,
18, forgered—ballsily enough—two "new" entire
plays of Shakespeare's, plus contracts, autographed receipts,
a sheaf of love letters (bound in a strip of ancient tapestry
torn from the walls of the House of Lords), and a document
proving Ireland's ancestor once saved Shakespeare from drowning.
Guess if a committee of the era's most distinguished scholars
lapped it up like honeywater. Boswell dropped to his knees
to kiss these artifacts and claimed that, having
seen them, he'd die happy now. But happiness,

scant hours after, is "fiddling in Venus's
concert-hall" with a Miss Septina Withers, actress. It's
easy enough to picture him, a grampus operatically huffing
around some spongy nook, then napping, then ragging
her dried patina off his noodley member—why
avert our gaze from something so honestly pursued?—but much
more difficult to steadily look as he's penning his letter
home to Margaret, filled as it is with the sweet *bon mots*
of fidelity. Our resolve in this world gutters
like a candle-flame. And that knife-crazy serial killer?—I

———

invented him. The bar, though, is real and so
is the woman. She's home now. Because she's an amateur birder
she laughs at those decoys (they aren't antiques but slipshod
plastic things that look like hiking boots with bills)
and then, with no transition, she's weeping, she's drunk
and she's weeping: no serial killer, okay, but still he was
a class-A asshole jerk. She turns the tv on: the President,
rerun for the country's insomniacs. She shakes her head
as if to clear it, then switches channels: the President again.
Let's visit her. She would say: "brood parisitism"

exists among ducks, and five other avian species;
the European cuckoo, for instance, replaces the eggs
of the warbler or thrush with its own, and it will duplicate
egg color and design for the birds being suckered. True,
the victim may discover this deception, then weave
a new nest over the cuckoo eggs—but just as often
the cuckoo simply repeats its trick: we've found nests seven
layers tall, the real, the fake, the real, the fake . . . *Now*
what's the President saying up there?—the soundproofed ovens
of Dachau? the vows to the Aztec and Sioux?

Sill Ritual: a survey

Cilley had died . . . Mary had rejected him . . .
And so they joined the miasmatic company of ghosts
that sworled his head and drizzled
into his writing. On July 23 of 1838, Hawthorne,
34 and requiring quiet and cleansing, journeyed
from Salem by coach and train to the thick-wooded
ridges and culverts of North Adams; and
on his first afternoon, having registered at the inn, he
hiked a narrow road through leaf-light, to a stream,
and stripped, and stretched out at full, in what he happily called
the "brawling waters." He would need this all his life.
"One dip into the salt-sea would be worth more
than a whole week's soaking," he'd later complain of the Concord,
though would submerge himself once or twice daily.

And entering the realm of the dead is a matter of water:
wizened Charon, poling his Plutonian raft,
the little dogteeth waves of the river slicing at its sides.
And reentering, back to the land of the living? . . . A bottle
of water was set at the stoop of our front door. I was
rawly-formed, 15. Death was new to me; all of its
confronting and euphemizing rituals, new to me. And
I watched—weary down to the filament, yes, but even so,
dumbly attentive—as my father tilted it, singing out
the Hebrew in his much grief-crinkled voice, and symbolically
rinsed from his hands the casket-touch,
the first skirled dust, the last adhesive dander,
of his mother's burial: *now* we could cross the sill,
back into some tentative version of normalcy.

But it doesn't need to be water: "Moses," says the Lord,
"draw not nigh hither, but first put off thy shoes from thy feet,
for the place whereon thou standest is holy ground"—and only
then, the Voice from out of the Bush reveals its blazing array
of injunctive and promise. And I think of the sprig one carries
for safepassage into a fairy ring's incomprehensible frolic, or
some secret word a bughouse inmate chants below his breath
each time he's returned to his cell, his sanctum . . . From
the vastitude of homogeneous space and time, we shape our own
small specialdoms by annunciatory units of just these
whispers, or clutches of myrtle, or sandals hesitantly stepped from,
left in shadow, while the Fire of God holds forth . . . So
no, it doesn't need to be water we declare
a boundary by. Nor does it need being "pure": I remember you

––––––

said you soaped your hands, each time, before finally leaving
the motel room: "under the lip of every cuticle, over
the webby parts between the fingers." Your "friend" must have had
his riddances, too. And also, check the register: your name
was different. In most ways, you *were* different six times every year,
out of town on the planet Convention: its different allowabilities,
and their un- and re-doctrination procedures. (Once, in the last
blurred hours of a French Quarter night, I sighted a room: a woman
swayed in her thigh-high snakeskin boots and her man was
kneeling, licking a leisurely snailtrack up the inside seams, and
they had titles for each other that, had their various colleagues overheard,
would be Venusian to them, or the language of bats; and then
they slept, I imagine, and woke, and exited over the edge of that
world for this other, in the early, borders-slurring New Orleans light.)

––––––

.

57

" . . . a huge pile of cotton bales, as high as a house . . . Barrels
of molasses, casks of linseed oil, iron in bars . . . Long Wharf
is devoted to ponderous, evil-smelling, inelegant
necessaries of life." In another three years, he and Sophia
will marry. For now, she stays behind in Salem. Hawthorne
notes his days away in tallies of salt and of coal,
a "measurer" at the Boston Customs House. He calms
the tirades of the work gangs. He counts gulls for sheep
in his boardinghouse bed. Some days the fog's as gray as soot,
as thick. And when his mail is delivered
at the docks, he quickly pockets-away Sophia's:
"I always feel as if your letters were too sacred to be read
in the midst of people—and (you will smile) I never read them
without first washing my hands."

"When wild beasts charge,

---

*Samuel Baker with deadly aim stops them in their tracks. Their
baggage animals die, their food supplies fail and they are reduced
to eating grass, fever lays them prostrate for weeks on end,
deceitful guides mislead them, hippopotamuses overturn their
boats, tribes attack with poisoned arrows, and they are never for
long out of hearing of the war drums. Through it all the
incredible Mrs. Baker never flinches. 'She was not a screamer,'
her husband tells us."*

arranged from Alan Moorehead and Ian Cameron

And in March of 1863, the men of their company mutiny.
Samuel Baker is facing over forty of the toughest roustabout louts
this side of the London docks, and every one of them
wants to abandon the Bakers here, on these foetid banks,
for the river water to soften them, and the claws of the African shadows
to have their instinctual way, and the sun, and the worm,
and the shears of the African beetle to bear them crumb by crumb.
Impulsively, Baker seizes the burly ringleader by the throat, and
in return "I had a crowd of men upon me," fists and teeth.
Can we just leave him there, as if this were a serial TO BE

CONTINUED***NEXT WEEK! and indifferently plod onward
toward the end of this poem: Modigliani, alone, and staring
dolefully at the shell-pink swells of a half-done nude . . . ?
Well, no; let's fetch the ever-plucky Samuel from this mess:
"Now as the scene lay only ten yards from my boat,
my wife, who was in the cabin ill with fever, witnessed the whole
affray. She rushed out, and implored me to forgive
the ringleader if only he kissed my hand and begged
for pardon." And such was her startling appearance there, that's
exactly what happened. Wow. We never tire of the story

of rescue, nick-o'-time, hair-breadth—of Lassie's
superolfactory senses, sure of the leak in the mine, and so
she tugs the child by his checkered sleeve to daylight.
Tell us Robin Hood, amaze us with the ladders and nets
of the firemen, the Four-Day Lucky Garlic Cure IT WORKS,
that Jewish infant hid from Nazi spies in the pit
of a slaughtered dog, that time Houdini unshackled himself below
a milky foot of river ice, or the Saviour in Whose love our foulest
underbrain desires are redeemed, if we accept Him . . . No,
we never weary of any of these. Listen—Amadeo Modigliani

was born July 12, 1884, when the family funds had slumped
to such a low that, as Eugenia Garsin Modigliani entered
labor, bailiffs entered the house to seize its furniture.
Remembering "an ancient Roman law which forbade the bed
of a woman in childbirth from being disturbed," the family
wackily heaped its prized possessions around the magic
pelvic drama taking place, and Amadeo was spasmed out
into a wonderful welter of red plush loveseats, a cupboard,
gilded knickknack shelves, and an escritoire. It's rescue,
rescue, rescue. But by 1915—31 years later—furniture

comes to this: the young art dealer Paul Guillaume
one evening passes the cottage where Modigliani and
Beatrice Hastings spent their turbulent loverstime together,
"he heard screams and bangs . . . As soon as he was inside the garden
he saw the couple hitting each other with chairs." And there's
hashish, and rum, flung cutlery, and one night Modi is witnessed
scratching plaster from his walls in a fit, then trying
to pull out the bricks. If it's extreme, we've all been somewhere
milder just as painful. What's that phrase
again?—*when wild beasts charge*. If tonight my wife

and I have been combatants, psychobabbling at the quick
of what we are together, hurtfully, while grouting drifted
down from the moon and grudges mounded up . . . you'll see
why I might want the Bakers in this poem, as totem mists
about us, curative, enabling . . . but must also add
this man in an attic. It's nearly dawn. His fingers are bleeding.
He stares at a half-done oil of Beatrice, lushly on her side
like a bottle of blush wine. In a little while, the thin plash
of the doorway sleepers peeing will announce another day
to cart his heart around in. *Now* what's going to save him?

The Title for a Collection of Poems
Appears from Out of Nowhere

The truth is, the world *is* flat
in that bleared, bearings-connoitering instant
after waking—everything's one perception backwards,
you too: thought is in a mildew
of earlier animal or fetal life, and your skin
isn't properly boundaried for a minute, it flimmers
out of itself like dry ice or the vapor of a jungle.
Often, just as all that falls away,
I think of viewing my Grandma Rosie
recomposed in her casket, maybe
like a painted cicada husk
left here, in this world, while the flying and chittering
lifted to another—which the rabbi promised happened
for a fact, and while I think a fact takes more
than merely petrifying faith, I do admit
that there are mysteries whizzing throughout an oxygen molecule
we haven't solved, and this makes the simplest breathing
multivalent. When I watch my wife
in sleep, and see the easy, rhythmic breaths
start catching, wadding in her throat with who knows
what dreamed fear, I understand nothing
ever occurs in a single universe only.
So a man will mumble "Everything's okay now" and be honest
and deceitful. A woman can care about this
and not. If we've been arguing, we do the mall
tonight to browse, act silly, and be alright
again. At the perfume counter we shpritz around
like naughty second-graders. The salesgirl
dabs a sample across my pulse and
I'd like to think I can feel its chemical

chains unforming as one wavy string of aroma rises
off the vein—the way it would be
if we could feel a prayer take leave of the body.
There might be the slightest pull,
as when a bandaid's lifted off of hair, and then
at least we'd know the truth.
The Truth, and other lies.

Adventures in Decipherment

1. Garbled

"They're so . . . *aggressive,*" you say.
(The new neighbors.) That's
good? bad? first
I need translating it, from the language I think
you speak, into a crude first draft of Albertspeak,
but already it's lost
in our weekly sitcom contretemps over who
lugs out the garbage bags this week. It turns out

I do. It's dusk, a regressively summerlike day
in early winter. Two ducks stump around
the garbage dump, the weather
and their migratory gyroscopes are talking this year
in opposing tongues. I linger outside.
It darkens. Through a set of ragged, gray-green teeth,
the moon is singing its garbled yet moving
Sanskrit to the waters.

2. Making Sure

"Sir Walter Scott, for instance, needed to explain
to his English readers such Scotch terms as
dour, daft, and *usquebaugh.*" It's good
to make sure. I imagine the Virgin Mary and Elvis
always repeat themselves, slooowly, in case
their words are too softened, *too* marshmallow-bodied
by long abeyance in the eternal, to be clear
in our hard and mortal air. And Rawlinson

dangled 160 feet above the valley floor
of Bagistana, "landscape of the gods,"
to copy its rockface's elegant ancient
Persian chiselwork, his lifeline rope diminished to what
appeared a thread in those miles of empty light
— "a methodical worker, he returned a year later
to check and then correct his copies on the spot." Like
saying *I love you* the second time, in case it didn't "take."

3. "Rosetta-sex,"

she thinks. There comes a time when every other dimwit
try at finding commonheld vocabulary fails;
after solo bouts of sulking burn the peevishness away,
the only wisdom to practice is slippery
skin on skin. Perhaps that's why the border quarreling
of nation-states continues to fatality, this
recourse being denied them. In any case, soon
he'll drag himself back in from doing the garbage, and

that dialogue of gland-&-*frisson*
begin. She thinks of when she was 9, a playmate
pumping his forefinger into an O his left hand made:
she blushed without even knowing why. But
we're all mutes at love, our top 10 tunes and
canon sonnets never coming close to the fishy accuracy
required: and so we'll speak our love like mutes,
with our hands; with our hands all over.

4. Americanese

is aburble, a stew of root and gluey marrowmeats
that's never done or fit on a 3 × 5 recipe card.
Kapeesh, you *shlemiel? mon* beautifully jiveass *cheri?*
Our most philologically dull still
easily breeze through polyglottish conversation,
bagel, mojo, glasnost, hoodoo, everyone *hablamos*
in a democratic roar. Accommodation
is no guarantee of permanence or clarity, however:

palooka is lost, *shilly-shally* is lost, I haven't hearkened
to *piccalilli* successfully uttered in years,
galoot, hooch, shutterbug, though they were living language
half-a-flash-of-time ago, on living tongues
that caked and cankered and slathered
passion upside other living tongues . . . *calliope*
or *Auschwitz* may as well be Tierra del Fuegan
by now, *sayonara,* Jackson, *ciao, adios.*

5. A Simple Night Scene

Lovemaking was over; the theory was love
remained. A person likes some reassurance, though
she was sleeping by now, and murmuring who knew
what encoded disclosures? Lightly, he touched his
head to hers; but, while he sensed the drowsy
hive-of-a-life in that intricate, sticky interior,
nothing articulate crossed—he could have been holding a stone
to his ear, listening for its physics. So

he dressed, walked out. The neighbors' house was lit.
It didn't seem to be eavesdropping, but a natural
extension of his day, that he should lean against their wall,
should tap whatever private Tagalog-for-two they
raged through various near-operatic gradations. And
he recognized their urgency—but not their words or
even the world of their words, they were so
otherly, scream-coarsened, so . . . so *aggressively* themselves.

The Two Parts of the Day Are,

first: I'm driving home when BOOMER cuts me off
with a tidily-clipped illegal left at Central & Oliver.
The Age of Lizards, the Age of Mammals, and now the Age
of Vanity Plates. AGNESJ appears from out of a cloud
of briquette-gray exhaust, and GRANNY, and KSSMYA.
A blonde woman in a t-shirt proclaiming her NATE'S
is piling her car trunk with monogrammed luggage, E;
her keychain flashes out DICK. It's depressing. And

second: Skyler greets me with the news that north
on Woodward, someone rode around the blocks this morning
shooting down people at random—pedestrians,
other drivers, nine in all who won't be coming home today
or ever. He was found with a bomb, an axe, and a beheaded
goose in his back seat. Nine people. Now they're just
the names being grieved in a few raw throats in this city;
on this planet; through the flux called Outer Space. The third

part of the day isn't day at all. It's night; and everywhere,
in the least of its creakings and beetle-jaws,
in the infinite zip of lepton and of quark
through what we like to think is "sky" but is burning and
emptiness, emptiness and burning . . . the night is saying
itself, in its language. I can't sleep. The moon makes silver
lace of my wife's unsheeted shoulder. And: SKYLER, I'm
whispering suddenly, like a 15-year-old at the fresh cement

—at the air, at the dark, at the thin lunar light,
at whatever of this world might read me.

Adonai and Company

The Gold Note Lounge and Boogie Palace

She was a smoky-throated eel-boned woman, that's
for sure; and, as she danced, the denim countermambo
of her hips implicated the whole of the room
—the women as well as the men,
knocked into a rapt daze by this
living faucet of sexual hotchacha. I remember
a thickly amber beer-and-bourbon slowness to the air,
that bar-air, you know it—like grimy honey. I remember
a note the sax held, it was a coalburning train's moaned o's
ripped straight down the middle. Something beautiful and sad
and ugly was going to happen, something very human,
with its licked lips and its bellyhairs, with its rinkytink
diversions and its handbills for the next week's band. But
now what we have is another slice-of-blues-and-lowlife exercise, when
what I wanted was something else entirely: outside,
the pebble lot is cool and gray. You only need to saunter
two, three steps away, and its surface is already smooth.
The city beyond is like that, too—its deeply-cratered griefs
and highstrung pleasures are, with distance, no more
grained than a lizardskin bag. Some highways. A dump. The rim
of slag plants. Then the plain itself, the muscular
redclay plain—below those stars
that burn in sky like its adrenalin. Then
foothills. Then, past even that darkly purple ruff,
the mountains—where the gods live,
Zeus and Aphrodite, Yahweh, Condor-Lightning-Flinger,
the whole gang. Their view is . . . well, to them
the icing-over of Lake Caudell is like the closing to bone
of an infant's soft spot. See?—there's no vocabulary,
anything we say is just a kneeling
on the wrong side of the door. Because

imagination fails in this, the gods
are bickering: who said what; who's fairest;
over the deed to Parnassian turf. Because imagination fails,
the gods are jealous tonight, deceitful, a few
have the yearning to fret alone and perfect a creation, the rest
are strutting like tycoons about their Olympian marble and clouds.
We feel this, far removed, as thunder or even the tumbling of seasons.
The gods are celebrating tonight, the gods
—we have no other words—are crowding their ballrooms
and bebop halls: the "dirty dog";
a doily-intricate waltz; the floor-whomping elephant hop.
We sense it this way: the heavens are charged,
the earth is crazed with subterranean bolts of seismic jitter, that
rumble the oils and fronds, and
whisper the earliest underlanguage
into our bodies, which emulate their respective deities then,
and we slick back our greased wings of hair
and enter our own night of dancing.

A Pantheon

The gods are out. The full moon films the damp skein
veining the cobbled back of a Nile croc. Tonight the gods
are apparent against the bric-a-brac of merely
mortal doings, are among us, are in form. Yes
even the ancient of gods—so here, along the slanting
banks of his representatives' slumber, Sebek

the Crocodile (sometimes Sebek the Falcon-headed Crocodile)
struts, and says our pain has a purpose, and makes all
of the other homiletic pronouncements appropriate to a god,
and nods as if almost bewildered himself at the storage of
resin-sealed crocodile corpses, or even individual
resined eggs: our worshipping is detailed and implacable. *Divine*

protection, James Holman called it, swimming to the African shore,
or tiptoe-circling Vesuvius's rim, while blind
—*deprived by the Almighty*, as his journals put it: and so
"protection" seems a proper redress. By the 1830s
he'd circled the world alone—whatever British
Christian Heaven he recognized, seeing him through

the overseen Earth of other gods—the gods that, with
the Yaweh of Jesus and Abraham, are out tonight. Poseidon
strokes his beard that on the vases repeats the hirsute curl
of seafoam stilled for a wine-imbiber's inspection.
Huehueteotl holds a freshly wrenched-up human heart.
The gods of thugees, of sherpas, of burghers, are

out, in total prowess tonight, bestowing their gaze
on the range of their various provinces, from the maximum
parabola a comet's fires define, to the least diameter
of the fetal esophagus summoned from its nub of salty
template-stuffs . . . The gods, and their labors, the gods,
and their inscrutable joys, are out. Now

having been our excuses for weakness and stupidity,
having been hated and feared, and having been adored
chorally and solo in every Indo-European language,
including glossolalia, including the one true esperanto
called silence: tonight, these old abstractions of ours
embody themselves, bemuscled, enfleshed: the gods

———

in their array are with us. The god of the hunt.
The god of lactation. The god of the nacreous chandelier
of frog's eggs gummed to the lily pad belly. The
clocktick 18th-century god created from empirical study
when Newton first undid the sun's
strict ribbon of color. These, and more. The god

of math, whose parallel lines meet only in infinity,
no less than the god of art, whose parallel lines meet
at the horizon. Loki. Vishnu. The god of the desert cactus,
for whom Rapunzel is one audacious flower set in a tower
of spikes. The god of the concentration camps.
The god of the lamb and the lion. And some

———

exhibit the wrath we know as their chiefmost attribute,
some random, some intentionally vengeful, depending
on whose the culture they serve and are served by; rats
eat into the nursery, hail in one night shatters
the fruits of the toil of ten months, pain is a fuse
through an arm then explodes in the chest . . . And some

76

are tender, infinitely milky and protective. One is
straightening a cripple. Some are incarmined by lust, are
sucking off the pure of heart in their sleep. The gods
of mercantilism are counting through eternity. The gods
of rarification are light divided by light then multiplied
by light to the highest power. To every people,

———

their gods. They enter us down to the oxygen-charge
on our red cells; and we're chastened, beat
like carpets, clean by the force of unbearable strength; or
we're exalted, I've seen children lift their crutches
up like wings at the bass in a gospel-lilted blues and
be weightless the length of a heartbeat; we're whatever

scripture-specific things we must be, when our gods are out.
In the sky. On the mountains. The oboist's god is the size
of the cathedral that's her nasal vault, and flutters there
like a hummingbird. The boxer's god fits bitten
in the dentifrice. Or there's finally a god so personalized he's
no god . . . 1830. James Holman. For all supposed

———

devotion, doesn't his intimate blackness, vast
and irreconcilable, swallow even a god? Well here
he is, his walkingstick in hand, and by pacing
the walls of the Kremlin, is measuring them exquisitely
to his universe one-person-large, and its needs.
We each have ritual like that. When I lived in Chicago,

in the gray lake air of the winter there, a blind girl
passed my house every morning, and tapped six times,
on six uneven wall bricks, with a mumbled name for each.
I never heard them quite, which is proper. Then I'd return,
say, to a stanza of mine, go step by step. Six
sticks, tick tick tick, tick tick tick.

A Refuge

doesn't need to be a physical place or even
of this world. Once,

up the all-too-straight, state-angling length of
35-North from Wichita, half-blind
with Kansas sun outside
and Goldbarth darkness inside, with
my life's small second wind at my back
and an ill wind dinning crossways
so the tinny 6-cylinder oomph of my travel
flickered like a match,
through fields the color of dead moth,
tasting dead moth on my tongue,
through dust, past stubble . . .

two deer
flew — I never saw their hooves hit down —
not 5 yards in front of my car,
from nowhere, from out of the blue,
yes and into the blue, although
blue didn't even exist in that grist-colored place
until their arrival. Surely
their bones were hollow. Then they were gone
as if dived into water: suddenly, completely, with
that quick splash of white tails . . .

and yet they seemed to hover there above the highway
for hours, my car approaching
for hours, my eyes at rest in the binary air
between them. I can't put in any words
what they reminded me existed in this life,

but: *deer* I hear somebody saying,

———

no: *dear.* I'm years back in a room
where a woman of fine-boned, almost mink-boned,
movement is
stroking me, in a wonderful way both
sexual and general at once. I feel safe here,
with these leaded windows softening the otherwise
bullying day, with time slowed down to her hands
making light lazy 8s at my nipples. I've paid
well for this, and there are certain words for her less
generous than mine. But she was there
when I needed — made of herself, and her room
with its scatter of hosiery floating like jellyfish,
a sanctuary, a few cash-only hours. When
I leave I'll wish that when she needs it someone's
there for her, and some shaped moment grows inviolate.
I even try to tell her how
I'm thinking of the church

———

the tour bus stopped at, in a village
in the olive country, yesterday. The group trooped through.
I lingered,
unable to turn from the hall where a woman was kneeled
in front of two stained glass panels of Eustace, 2nd century
saint — the one out hunting who encounters a stag
with a miniature, speaking Christ between its antlers.
It was easy to see: this woman was hurt, inside, and close
to empty. Light entered the dim stone hall through the windows,
two huge arms of light
with their colorful sleeves rolled up, and
in those capable and extraterrestrial hands she
let herself be held — with everything else, just then,
inconsequential. How

———

must it have been, in the woods, with winter
steaming away through the dazzling cabochon sides of the river,
and bloodlust
billowing over the hounds, the air as dark as a linseed varnish,
birdsong—every bird, on one note—quieted . . .
Eustace stares at the stag. At the living
mitre it bears. I think he must have been tormented
for years, and now here was a moment out of the bounds
of spacetime, out of the clamoring battle of gut
and psyche like serpent and mouse, a moment simply
rubbed free of all bothersome detail, so made
weightless . . . For hours, he stares. I see him
softly start to speak. And then,

like any deer, it bolts for cover.

Alveoli

There are some 300 million alveoli in the normal human lung; if spread out flat, their total area would add up to 750 square feet, or all the floor space of an average house.

arranged from Guy Murchie

Who *are* these unsung perpetrators of Taj Mahals
and racecourse tracks and Neptune-orbiting NASA missions,
figured from the sanctum-nooks of my body? Engineers,
linearists of fingerprints unwhorling
into razor-straight surveyor's lines
by which the paving-stones of famous ancient plazas
might be set, The Great Wall, Hadrian's Tomb.
And: "if the capillaries of every man and woman
of Caesar's Rome became components of a straight line, then,
when compared to the total length of that city's plumbing . . . "
And: "if all of the cubic volume of the small intestine's villi
were placed on a pedestal in the Louvre . . . " We seem to need these
sly confabulators of metaphor, we seem to need comparing
what's familiar—Niagara, the Hanging Gardens of Babylon,
the face of the moon—with something so puzzlingly strange as our lives.

One normal human body fits inside
one normal iron lung. It's a simple statistic.
Even its motion is simple, really: in, then out.
And Emily's death at 34 was simple,
complicated and simple and preordained
the first time she gagged up the mealy bolus of cystic fibrosis
ooze, still slick with the red smear of birth.
The machinery keeping her breathing
throbbed the floor, like a foundry's, or a submarine's.
My wife (her sister) watched. The second-hand skinned time

81

as if the clock were an apple. Everything: simple,
orderly. First, the light in a single room of her oxygen
failed. Then another room went out, and another.
Finally, the last small lamp; the whole house,
dark now, empty.

———————

At Carnival, the streets of Rio overpour with partying:
tissue-and-wire Fire Dragons a block long, nudie conga lines . . .
you get the feeling Rio could double in size and still the merriment
would spill across its brim . . . The same with sadness; or even
the thinner emotions: wistfulness, say. There isn't any
meaningful unit of measurement. One night I walked
alone to where the park lifts into an oak-crowned knoll.
What was I?—hurt? contemplative? something
poetic like that, something poetic and human like that.
What was I, but a heart driven out of the body
on its pulmonary wings? Don't tell me you haven't ever felt this
hagiography of the breath. You sigh,
the length of an armbone. You sigh, and it reaches
to Venus and back. You breathe, you set them
end to end, Versailles, Old Faithful, the Halls of the Gods.

Stories

Betsy Nelson of Arlington, Va., sued Irving's Sports Store of nearby Falls Church after security personnel there falsely accused her of shoplifting a basketball. Nelson, 33, was nine months pregnant.

as reported in *National Lampoon* "True Facts"

Still, it's best to check. The sly, diversionwise practitioners of contraband
are legion: no grimed particrumb of swag escapes consideration, no
seam of concealment. "A mouthful of wadd
is a day's wage," went the wisdom in the Borrowdale mines—wadd
being graphite, "also called *kish* or *kellow* or *black-cowke*," this specific
British version being singularly pure to such degree, the miners entered
by a trap-door, stripped, changed clothes, and after six subterranean
    hours
reversed this process "under the wary superintendence of the steward,
    who
is armed with loaded blunderbusses," often his underling grubbing
up "suspiciously-carriaged bumholes." Plus, the saint in the story

Jeanine tells, whose cadaver its proprietary Church refused to parse
as separate relics; when some Princess asked a special, solo, confessional
few minutes in its chamber, she was granted this request; so now
we'll leave her, as she wished it, in that candleflicker privacy.
The story that concerns us is an infant stitched inside the plucked-clean
ribcage of a dog; the widened rectal hole let enough of his minimal
pushbolt of oxygen in and out. But what if he wailed, even
through the sluggish veils of sucked wine? Yes, or what if simple random
    malice
slipped an image of toying around with the dead dog into the bored
    heads
of those slow-wit S.S. border guards? It worked, though; and

83

in fact he slipped as readily through the Jew-check at this station as he
slipped the day before between the antipodally-widened thighs
of his mother: no less universes-exchanging a matter of inches. They
go o-mouthed so assuredly that first time at the nipple (even "helpless,"
as we see and need to see them, they're so smoothly neural-programmed)
that it's clear the first, the matrix, of our tasks is smuggling: much
the way the thimblebrain inside a newborn tern's skull is a 3-D star chart
fired, in the egg, with the astronomical chandelier that takes it,
weeks old only, from northern Greenland winging to the South Pole. We
arrive here, primed in passage-blood, already possessing the lore we later

call religious mythology, spiritual aspiration, yes and the stink
of our possum-hole fears, not to mention the tasseled satin corset
and muscle-tee of our chemical-written agenda of sexual beckoning:
     all of it,
in us so it *is* us, from a Somewhere where the bossed plush of the
          night sky
and the circuitry of nerve-ends touch, a page of instructional text
en face with a page of its illustration. This is poetry-twaddle,
however. Our story is here in this room, in plain suburban daylight.
1991: two sides of a family gather. The *mohel* lifts his little
slicer-of-a-tool, then gives his ritual sufficient flick at the stem:
a *bris*, a bunch of cousins and much chablis, and a grandfather

telling the tale *he* was told, of his long hour in the swaddling-meats
of a slaughtered dog, when he was this old. What are we
but these stories we unspool? A life is stories the way a pencil is
70 miles. *Pencil*. . . I'm back to those wretches clucking a stub
of Borrowdale writing-lead under their tongues, a pretty penny
on the market. Or here: she's regally departing down the ornate ranks
of priestly observation, nodding dutifully to each damn clerk, then
          through
the gate, and dashing from the shadows where I've stashed her, falling
crazily at the feet of her friends, and ekeing out, in its coat of her spit
—gnarled as a radish, the color of verdigris—the big toe of a saint.

Thawed

On the hottest day for its date in the city's history, I fall asleep
on the ice-pack I'm using for minor lower back pain, and I wake
(with Charles Dickens still in hand) to see I'm frostbit
over an area about the size (and the crystalline feel)
of six or seven popsicles inserted under my skin. It looks as if
I could tap, and the small of my back would crack like a cheap ceramic.
It's 86° outside — the emergency room is astonished at this
unseasonal touch of the arctic; if I'd crawled in already
giving birth to a litter of rabbits I'm not sure I'd occasion more
enormous-eyed response. For days thereafter, I find myself
reading the mishaps of early polar explorers, stuck
to the devolvement of their narratives by a sick fascination as surely
as zero degrees sticks tongues to metal. They can't pry me loose. I'm
there when Mertz, in a spasm of madness, chews his own
         frostbitten finger
off and spits it out; when Mawson pitches away the detached soles
of his own feet; and when Scott notes Oates's feet
have blackened and split like a bad banana, and the rest
start dropping tufts of frozen hair and the leathery petals
of frozen fingernails behind them. You can't be fooled
by photographs of respite — penguins crowded about
for "Waltz Me Around Again, Willie!" as it blossoms in that hard air
from an Edison Patented Phono-Graph; no, when the blizzard drove
         down,
Shackleton's men were savaged by frostbite
"even in their sleeping bags." These are sections of stories
of such heroic questing, such determination, they seem to be
by-products of a greatness, manufactured
in those lands of spectrally beautiful white on white,
crevasse and glacier, places where even lichen can't live; my own
fifth-rate affliction isn't lessened, but ennobled, by attachment

that I force on these magnificoes of suffering, gaunt
step by step, and suddenly I understand the faddish rash
of celebrity-level confession-fest tv has become,
and the popular press, that up till now eluded me:
Victoria Vavoom was abused by a cousin, and wants to pour
her story out of her shimmering minnow-like designer gown
for the audience millions: Studley Mann had a mother
who drank, and wives two, three, and seven cheated: even
the Baronet Genoise Torte St.-Burgundy the Third admits
such pissy, maggoty fears, such ursine hungers, such
a locked-up closet of victimhood, we understand he's
everyone, albeit he can afford to inscribe his story
in gold dust skywriting if he chooses. Now our miseries,
our formerly pennyante and shameful miseries, are bridges
to their likeness in the lives of the grand; the pain we bore,
intolerably huge but hidden in us, now, at last, is paid
its proper magnification. I return to Dickens
with clarified vision. Every back-hunched factory boy
at shift's end, weary in toe-bone and ear-bone and tail-knob
so that even the calcium forming in his body
shrinks at the thought of another day, and then
he's thumped with a brass-base candlestick, to boot—is
singing my smidgeon of labor across the pages of Art.
Each fallen lady of high estate, who wakes
pawed-over greasily by canalmen, in the shadows of the bridge
she'd come to rest beneath, between the rains—is
making of my fishbait-weight travail a burden
worthy of the tears of Victorian England. Deep in me,
where they'd been frozen shut, my slivers of A-through-Z distress
are thawed and rising, are here in my palms
I hold up unto the heavens tonight, and ask the gods
to witness such enormity of human hurt
that their only response could be compassion,
searing my flesh with a lightningblast
so fierce, so otherworldly, it heals.

Not to Contravene

=====

It could be that a human being is no more than the genes' survival machine, their vehicle into the future. Whatever is best for the genes, we do.

article in a science journal

. . . the "Bird's Head" Haggadah, *in which the artist illustrated the story of the Egyptian enslavement, the Exodus and the details of the Passover ritual with figures having bird heads instead of human heads, in order not to contravene the traditional injunction against representing the human figure.*

Abram Kanof, Jewish Ceremonial
Art and Religious Observances

Dear Cousin,
      So you remained. If you remain
yet, this will come to you in the lapis-and-calfskin casket
with the other, more official, history
sent by courier back to the Courts of our Depradation
to say hello; or goodbye; or to crow
emboldened by the sweetness of our settlement after
so much thorn and sword and retch-in-the-baskets; or
simply to heal the wound of the few of you who
stayed.
      If you were right to, you with the date-purple-blush
at your throat-ruffle, golden dove-eye you, and
fit to be a braceleted and rose-bathed monthly consort
for their sanctum priests—now
you know best. I only want to say that I was faithful
for a year; then it was 39 more; I have grandchildren now,
they sleep with their beaks like small tents
watch-fires wash deep orange against an indigo night! So
I have written this in boasting

and apology; I remember our games in the rubble,
the first fine wine-colored down across your sex
we dampened; and mine; and I have been true to that
emphatic urge, but not to you.
                    Oh, God,
and there is only the One, my cousin, was with us! Heaven's
sediments fall to this world in a Column,
dark, a cloudiness, but cold to the touch as if marble
—or so we remember it now. I touched it,
I was 20 and nothing could stop me,
and my palm was stung by a hundred stars
that traveled through the flesh like burning gnats
among the handbones and out the other side—I tell this
to my little ones. The Column led us. At night it was
a fire and it led us. We were ragged and empty and verminous
but not lost. And when we quarreled, then
the Jays would intervene, for this is the way of their tribe,
and hold one of us, and peck—I saw an eye
burst, yes, so near me that its threads and jellies shattered
on my arm. But order was kept. And when the embers
died and the few milk-goats were quiet in their bundle,
then the Nightingales sang, by the lutes
they use whose strings set off the strings in a person's chest,
the way a daughter will cry when the mother is crying,
and so we all cried, sweetly, softly, all the tribes in song,
you know this is the way of us all.
                    The Sea
of Reeds? You wonder. But we walked across. The waters
parted, they made two walls and a passageway and we
walked across. With living fish and eels set
like carvings in those walls! Of course
your masters followed. Their whip guards followed.
Their shitsnake pighound whip guards followed. Did one
escape to tell? They were caught like ants in a scroll
rerolling. The waters were that
cleanly edged: like a scroll. And for a day we heard
the ghosts of their wails behind us.

                              Then
didn't we dance! And make a fatbacked bull burnt offering to
the One. The Grackles, ever our cleverest warriors, were sorriest
we had no chance to test ourselves against the enemy host
with shield and club, so danced the fiercest to dance that
temper away. And the Larks, with their little clown steps,
to divert them . . . But all of us, merry, and our rags
as good as banners, with our cowbone flutes and tambourines,
and one plump Quail maiden with her cloth undone
by frenzy, and nipples as brazenly raised as figs, though
I thought only of you, my cousin, and even,
in those days, how you might yet leave the Courts with a band
of stragglers so to catch up.
                              Oh I was exultant! And
I saw how I was wrong—some few of the stars of the Column
had lodged in my body, had not passed through,
had snagged like burrs in the meat of me; I felt them,
in my exultation, sparking through the darkness of
my head, and chest, and loins. That night,
as we marched by the muscles of light that filled the Column,
I saw how *it* needed *us*—what would it be,
without our weary, serial column of following? without our
bloodrushed quick to embody its sparks? The angels of God, and
there is only the One, my cousin, would be—without us—
like weather without a world.
                              The deprivations
started—you will understand, who knew the barbed lash of the overseer;
but this was the lash of the sun; who knew the hunger
of an empty trough; but this was the hunger of empty land;
and sores the size of a child's hands on our bodies,
and a thick yellow run from our lips; I will not speak
of the worms. And then the miracles
started—and these, too, you will understand, from having
been there in the Days of our Deliverance: the rain of frogs,
and locusts, and the rest. And so a dew of food
awaited us, some mornings; and that Hawk who led us struck
a desert stone and water poured forth.

And even so,
the first oasis was the first true cool, and bathing, and leaf,
in a year. We named it Blesséd Green, and dallied a moon
to a moon there. She was bent to fill a clay pot at the pool,
and once again her fig-tipped rises made a sexual skin of the very
air I stared through—my Quail, my buttery-buttocked
Avianne, who is beside me now with the young of her young
all peeps in her lap. I could not guess that, then; but only knew
you were a year away; and she was plump and distant by a hand's span,
yes, or less; and she flourished her naked flesh at the nape
where the head-feathers first surge lushly out . . . And so I
stroked her there—both skin and feathers rose—and broke
my vow to you. For there are other contracts being alive
means; and we were a People first on our way to fulfilling of these,
and plenty, and increase of plenty, were part. In this my shame
and happiness are twined—and that is all of what I need to say,
my cousin, to you, this long time since.
                              I hope you do
well; I wish you no ill for your rootedness there in the land
of tears and mortar; if you flower in such bitter soil,
amen. But you are truly of the Gathered Tribes
no longer, for the Tribes are something else; and I will let
that other history ribboned alongside this
—our exodus and joy—recount the Hawk upon the mount,
and the Law, and the seraph-cornered Ark, and all the prayers
and knives by which we won our place
the One had promised. It is a rich, rough land
He chose; as we are His Chosen; as we are His
                                        flock.
And if I walk among the hills on certain evenings, and
remember . . . twisting my bill in your bill,
clipping our feathersweat faces together . . . I will tell you
something. There are Powers
that require us, and move us, so
to move themselves; for we are the ways
by which they solve their problems. And if they are giant
Columns, sized to a nation, filling the sky; and
if they are stars no larger than sesame seeds
at the heart of the pit of the flesh we are—no matter, they

are the same, my cousin, you
with the date-purple blush at your throat-ruffle,
golden dove-eye you.
                        Perhaps your master asks
who was your first love; this is from that
                                        one.

Architectural

When the King of the Gypsies was buried
they lined up picnic tables for three city blocks
through the cemetery, eating roast pig
and downing flagons of wine, and trying to hustle
the contract for paving over the cemetery main drive.
And there's that tombstone in Paris: the dead man,
cast life-sized, and women wishing
to be pregnant visit to rub his bronze crotch.
Ghosts appear in every culture,
terrifying the living with cliché chains or
aiding the living with cliché moaned advice,
but one was reported driving a rose-pink Caddie
up the interstate: I like that.
Angels. Sphinxes. Admonitory skulls.
Whatever. I'm trying to think of death
a new way—as something not final,
as something to face
that does have a face of its own. You know
the way that children believe if it isn't visible,
in front of them, it's ceased to exist
—is dear, but wrong.
I'm trying to see in the other rooms now.
"Afterbirth," we say, though
that's completely wrong of course.
In one of the other rooms it was there long before.

The Voices

1. Paged

The dead will speak through anything.
Give them a rock and they'll call it a PA system.
Give them light and they'll fax.
The new dead are teetering
dextrously on the legbones of the old dead,
like stiltwalkers, summoning us to their powwow
in circles of chalk and foxfire and lime. The dead are
tapping out morse on their kuncklebones,
are rattling (maracas), shivering (sistrums), though no one
metaphor ever suffices, the dead are flashing their millisemaphore
out of the poplar's disjunctive bough.
What we call memory, anyone
once called ghosts: they know your name,
your dreams are their calling your name
in choric cut-and-paste recombination.
There's that country where a flock of ibises shirring the sky
is something like a sentence being diagrammed. The air
is the dead's; it *is* the dead, resimplified to particle and wave,
and we grow jittery at this, jittery, having learned
from the perfect Chinese vase and the sonnet: form
should close itself with grace and finality. Studying
the John Deere backhoe go at the ground for another grave,
the industry of it, the plain hard fact of the casket,
it's impossible to think of anything other than nothing,
nothing nothing nothing, in that clayey earth. The mouth
must be among the first of our softnesses to crumble . . .
Afternoon. Ohio. Heat. You
pass by a stone and the summer air is
humming around it. You're being paged.

2. Nuts

"Not this one, this is junk . . . THIS one!"
—my friend Bob Lietz is lifting an intensely coral fountain pen
with a marbled girdle of celadon-green, from a weltered-up tray
of inferior others. Slowly, this week I'm visiting him
in the slumbering swales of hicksville Ohio, I'm beginning
to see these 60-year-old beauties—these neglected
panatellas and cheroots of yesterwriting—through his zealousness:
a burgundy laminate Maxima Vacumatic,
a Duofold Lapis Blue and a Duofold Mandarin Yellow,
a Montblanc filigree Spider-and-Web, and the rest . . . It
isn't the money (although there's wheelingdealing by
the oodle: a Parker Aztec goes for $10,000), "They're
lovely," his voice pressed thin by the weight, the sweet
and intimate weight, of this observation, "and people . . . "
he searches, and settles, half-satisfied only, on "*cared* so much."
I've seen him lost inside the lustrous finish of a blue-black cap
for fifteen nearly-sacramental minutes. Later,
the long lawn and its scumbled heads of clover growing
shadowy with dusk: "This might sound crazy
but some of these pens, they're telling me stories
about their original owners. I live with the pens for a while,
I get glimpses from those earlier lives. Here—" one
is engraved HON NYLAND DARBY. "*Hon,* you see?
The Honorable. He was a judge, I think a hanging judge
of the old school. Over time I'll know more." He sees
my look. "I *told* you it's crazy." Maybe. I think
of the canes of the blind, defining an alien world, and how
tonight Bob might be holding a pearl Wahl Deco-banded,
figuring out the details on the other side
of the greatest darkness. "Some pen collectors are *really* nuts."

3. Ghost-Mouth-Home

The bowls are scored in a ritual design
"whose meaning is lost in far antiquity" — we guess,
though, that this diamonded pattern means
a net: a something to catch, then hold. The bowls
are filled to the lip with cistern water, and
then brought by the shaman (sometimes
today, it's a priest) to a consecrated mud-brick hut
on the high plains, where a set of rough-cut jalousies
slits the winds. The water's surface feathered
north-to-south means such-and-such; east-to-west,
a different reading. These are the ancestors
speaking. There are endless combinations of repeated
disturbance, glisten, duration, force; the dead
have many homiletic comforts and admonitions,
it turns out the dead are breezy old coots. Well
why *shouldn't* they be? — the living are yammering
daylong, from their first ass-slapped bewailing to
the last of their deathbed natter ("come close, the gold
is buried in . . . *gghhhk* . . . "), with any number
of Creative Writing Workshops stuffed between,
their flags of self-expression flapping ("*I'd*
make that 'yapping'") over the labor of all of those
sovereign-states-of-one. Meanwhile, the sun
is lush in the east; the hut of the ancestor bowls,
the "ghost-mouth-home," is glowing like an ingot
in that undiluted touch. The goats are rounded up,
and the kitchen-embers are coaxed into flame,
and the children are marching chattering
into their poetry writing class the teacher
back from the city started this year.

4. Primitive Engine

All afternoon and half into dusk, a man and a woman have hurt
each other, using words like horsewhips—when he thinks of it
in this way, he can see the cruel exactitude: that brutal force
into the handle, then its delicate translation at the fine and
damaging tip. He sits there, watching dusklight moil inside
the dust of the road with a sedimentary thickness. Nothing's
clear. That morning, he sentenced a fellow for stealing a horse,
a constant offender, a snake-eyed son-of-a-b. This thief was
the size of an ox, and cried like a kitten. Only now, with
day's-end light in his auburn two inches of whiskey,
does he question his decision. "My client had every right to consider
the roan his property"; "Your Honor, I object—the bill of ownership . . ."
and so on, into the usual murk the truth becomes under anything
over a single gaze. And who is the High and Mighty Nyland Darby
to pass stern judgment—eh?: a man who's made his wife
cry down black lightning from the sky, to fry them both
clean off the Earth. With one more whiskey-inch, her waterfall
of red hair, and the strawberry-roan of the mare, will mix
in a sickly sugary way that knocks him weak to his knees,
dry-heaving . . . *then* what would his grandfather think, surveying
this sorry world from his august oil portrait? The first
robed representative of the Courts to preside in the county, and
to this day no one man more just has graced that bench . . . He
doesn't swig his third inch from the bottle, though;
he's only had enough to lift the Old Man's quill pen nimbly
from its crystal well—the locally-famous "sentencing pen."
It's beautiful, isn't it? All of that weightless faery substance
framing a central rectitude. The more he holds it,
strokes it, as if charging a primitive engine, the more the Old Man
fills the room then clears his throat.

5. When the Word Is Whispered

An amateur rockhound's cracking a basket's likeliest
gray candidates, but—nothing nothing nothing . . . / "This
statue is basically wicker, decorated with metal buttons.
At full moons, 'the lean ones'—their lineage of kings going back
at least 16 generations—communicate through it." / *. . . nothing*
still, and nothing; but then . . . / "The goddess's temple-devotee
lifts the viper, flings it to the tiles, and in its writhing esses
reads deific prediction." / *. . . the final split reveals a perfect*
fern in the center, each rung of it eloquent. Quite the granite
raconteur.
⠀⠀⠀⠀⠀⠀⠀My father is dead, and while I sense him
in the air sometimes—a kind of psychic jacquardwork
I've weaved of sun and oxygen—I've never heard one syllable
of post-interment jibberjabber. "Yes" or "no" would work
on almost any occasion; given *my* ability to face temptation,
"no" reiterated once a day or so, and only "no," would do just fine
—one lousy sound you'd think an elm could utter,
given infinite time and infinite wind (both are). But
I've visited Lietz in Ohio; from now, I'm going to keep my ears
emotionally skinned, and when the word *is* whispered up that parfait
shale and bitumen, the dime-sized gong-bones are going
to boom. I've seen Lietz cleaning the cases of Schaeffers of his
with all of the care of a Vatican artisan giving a final chamois-shine
to the rose-marble pizzles of putti. Yes and I've
witnessed him bearing a good day's collecting
out of the junk shop's mausoleum-like gloom, and into
the ordinary leafy light the car was parked in,
dancing like mad, and I've heard him
saying (maybe not in these words, but saying) this is the gold one,
this is the chosen one, this is the nib that will save us.

The Book of Speedy

The Book of Speedy

1.

The far trees bristle up like a hairbrush.
Overhead, the sky is a wan blue.
Two clouds look as if they're sharing
cellular material through a mutual wisp. I suppose
we could speak of the sex of clouds,
their combinative ways,
their freight, their fume-edged separations. We
could speak of ourselves through anything
really, any mask or mannequin our happenstance provides,
komodo dragon, moray eel,
laser surgery, pee from a rocketship freezing and
circling Earth forever, rain, no rain,
the rotunda skullbones of whales,
the chain-gang ants in the grass . . .

———

The universe
wants to talk to us, I'm sure of that,
it wants to and it does,
though we perceive it as the white talc
over thumb-plump purple grapes,
as the shakos of dust below the bed,
the umber fronds of rust up a bumper.
Even the universe's most stentorian proclamations . . .
it isn't the hog hit broadside,
it's the dusklight in the rearview mirror
dwindling to a needleprick.
                    The High Gods
are my theme here, or whatever
psychic monologues, or everwiffling red-shift edge

of energies we call "the Gods"—but
fallen, from such aboriginal nebulousness,
to language:
            something common and
salival, something, anything, though
by that I mean the Gods have been recorded as speaking
as well through thunder and fiery orbs
as the picked-apart scat of the peacocks.

———

"The tree that I was thinking of was one we always stopped to look at. Often
there was a black donkey tethered to it. When the donkey opened wide its
jaws and brayed it made the most tremendous heehaw, it was like the
creaking of the door of the world. It was much too big a sound for a donkey
to make, it was as if something else was making itself heard *through* the
donkey."

2.

Among the stunted duns and tans
of the print tacked up above his study desk, the donkey
is lavender-black; the woman at the well,
while based in grays, is fleshed in umber-pink, and
even the clay of the jar she holds against this background drabness
shows the rosiness of life—she holds it
upright on her shoulder like a tiny child lifted there
to better see a parade. The woman, the animal,
the mouth of the jar, and the relatively cavernous mouth of the well
would have a four-way conversation
for the proper person, each a different Biblical passion
rendered, from the bedrock of this uninviting landscape,
into speech, into perhaps—who knows?—prodigious,
chthonian, luminous speech; but not
now and not here: not for him.

_____

"*Jee*-zus," he'd muttered. "Oh
just don't give me any of that Jesus shit," she'd
spat back, "*money* is your God."
That was a year ago.
                              Now
he's reviewing the tax shelter's rolled-over funds,
and the dividends. Was she right, that day?
She's in the bedroom, the door closed: some kind of burbly
synthesized music leaks out.
The boy's in the playroom, kabooming and zooming, POW!,
with his plastic figurines and tacky gag shop items.
It's a happy house, isn't it? Almost
blessed. Devotionally, he tic-tac-toes
six-digit figures into his pocket calculator, thus
calling them down to shush around benevolently
in the calm night, on their greenback wings
—his Lord's host of pecuniary angels,
the Angel of Daily Compounding, the Angel of Wall Street . . .
he can hear their rigid, numerical madrigals.

_____

The boy's in the playroom, kabooming and zooming about.
KASHMOOSH! He's four. His (chewed-on) Captain Cosmo figurine
is headquartered in his *Captain Cosmo Choco-Drink for Lunch* mug.
That's the good guy. The bad guy is Borneo Joe the Wrestler
who lives in the Tiki-God mug that his parents brought home
from Tiki Gardens Dinner and Drinks. In alternation,
Joe and C.C. decimate each other—WHOARRR!—with dropped
eraser bombs and lobbed salvos of broken-up crayons, one
of the primary pleasures of being four. I'll tell you
                                                    this
about the ethereal tether that, though thin, still
links our lives to timelessness. The Gods
—the unimaginable patterns in the atoms of stars
and nervous systems—need to be imagined; we
provide them Masks: Ahura Mazda, Mithra, Jehovah, sometimes
sculpting lesser masks for *these* Masks: out of soapstone,
coral, marble, clay-with-seeds-and-pig-tusks . . .
Sandalwood was the material for Hawaiian gods,
like *ku-kaili-moku*, the "eater of land," but
trade, and visiting Christian missionaries,
halted the production of these ancient holy images
by the early 19th century. "Today,
Hawaii is visited by millions of people hoping to find reminders
of a Polynesian paradise where unspoiled people once lived
beside idyllic lagoons. So the tourist trade has fitted out
the old gods with new names and bogus legends. These
are called 'tikis,' a Maori name
that has nothing to do with Hawaii . . . " *Tiki*
party lights in red, white, green and yellow,
Tiki key chains, pop bottle openers, vases . . .

———

How do you measure the fall of a God to Earth?
In units of bathos.

———

104

SCHWACK!
one excellent souvenir Tiki mug in moss and chocolate glazes,
in pieces—uh-oh. This is a price paid
in our endless war against the forces of darkness.
Oh, he knows there's good and evil, it's just that
evil for him is a cartoon man with mellerdrama sneers
inked in. He doesn't understand it can be corporate,
that people somewhere hate his father for merely
institutional allegiance. He doesn't understand, not
yet, the ways that tragedy can be the size of a node:
                                        his mother's
in the bedroom, the door closed. Goopy synthesized music
washes over her rolled-up body in waves, in nearly
oceanic waves, and what she'd like to be is something
smooth and fetal heaved up on a beach. So she could start
over then, without the cancer. Shhh. She hasn't told him
yet, she's waiting until he's done for the night
with his goddam stock market pedantry, yes or maybe
she won't tell anyone at all: the radiation therapy
will work, it *will* work, then this momentary flaw
in her system can be her secret. "Radiation"—whatever
that is. It's her religion for now, as difficult
to picture as the subtleties and precepts of religion, and
the mask that makes it personal for her
—she can't help it, she knows it's a joke—is the logo character
used for years in his company's advertising campaigns:
the beaming bulb head and zigzag voltage body
of Mr. Light-Brite. "Hey! All day and night,
It'll be all right . . ." (and then he tips
his zillion-watt derby) " . . . With *LIGHT*-BRITE"—his tune,
his mnemonicy tune she needs so much to believe in.

————————

"These are our modern mythological figures, avatars of Another Plane:
Smokey the Bear; Elsie the Cow; Mr. Clean; Snap, Crackle and Pop; the
talking Kool-Aid Pitcher; Speedy Alka-Seltzer. These are the icons, like it or
not, of Cleveland and Pocatello and Philly and Jacksonville. And under their
trademarked, tutelary scrutiny, with the cultic theme-music and slogans
appropriate unto each, the organizing rituals of our American days take

place. The Dutch Maid Cleanser Girl is helping us, in advantageous units measured by single scrubs, to keep back the legions of disarray and besmirchment. Charlie the Tuna (tuna), Tony the Tiger (corn flakes), and the M-G-M lion (movies) remind us: once we lived as equals among the Animal Powers, only later shaped them to our Neolithic needs, and in our blood we keep in vibratory concert with them yet. I mean this tongue-in-cheek—and seriously as well. For who are we, to say their presence functions less than mythologically because their other purpose is commercial? (Isn't any religion a part of its economic times?) Yes, who are we to say to the supplicants thronging at various niches and altars: this mouth is an oracle, this one not?"

3.

And the future is read in the slippery knots and inclines
of the raw lamb liver: Deity
has written in the liver, where a few will claim to understand
a language otherwise spoken in effluvia, photons, and genes.
And the future is read in lees, in heated cracking tortoise shells,
in cast beans . . . *Divination*:
                              the divine
rising out of our marketplace stuffs and shuffling its
schoolroom flash cards. *This is the moon,*
the cock, the coffin spider, the cesium atom . . .
repeat after Me.

_____

Once, sitting in on anatomy class, I saw
an intern stretch up fatty strings from the torn-open purpled dough
of a woman's body and, an impish seizure,
tauten them with one gloved hand
to play them with the other. Not
that there was really any sound, except I remembered,
when I was a child, seeing the distant shapes in a room
through the vibrating side of a harp.
                              The lesson,
the music lesson, is everywhere.

_____

"Of composts
shall the Muse disdain to sing?" James Grainger
simply asks: *The Sugar-Cane, a Poem,*
his 18th-century verse treatise
on efficiently running Jamaican sugar plantations.
Johnson's critical response is droll,
of course, and Boswell reports a performance at Reynolds's house
one night occasioned witty scoff; but, still . . .
the slipknot signatures of flies in the air around it . . .
then a season, another season, and then the earliest

pale-green shoots of the sweetness . . .
Grainger knows where in a person
murmurs of poesy oft first stir their effects. "Now,
Muse," he continues, "let's sing of rats . . . "

———

I once heard a blues harmonica player
insist his soul was in his spit.

4.

Thunder
breaks out of the deeply fulminous clouds . . .
Then later, nascent sun breaks through . . .
And when a Tiki mug—SCHWACK!—breaks? . . .

---

then Jiffy Boy yodels his famous Sponge-It-Up jingle, bows once, and
nimbly glissades (on jet-blast rollerskates) down a mountain of glop and
rubbish toward our own telltale mess: his eyes, like cat eyes in a car's beams,
are electrified henna; he has the dancing fantods, in excitement over the
mopping ahead; his hands, in fact, are whisk-brooms, and his torso is a
scouring pad. He lives with Mr. Zip (the Post Office), Little Oscar (wieners),
and The Chicken King (cluck cluck). And Betty Butane (with those ooh-la-
la red lips and inky lavish lashes) has a gas flame for a head, and so is
perpetually her own natty wimple, plump and bunsen-blue. And Skweezme
is a tarantella-frantic roll of paper towels. The Keebler Elf presides over
cookies. Mr. Goodbuy, Mr. Goodwrench, and Mr. Goodmeat each is the
potent genius of his domain, and has it bad (I mean the spasmic cardiac
pitterpat of sexual yearning) for Penni Wise, and Cora Gated, and Bar-
B-Cutie, and maybe even the bluesy chanteuse for The California Raisins
(raisins). Need I belabor the dapper, top-hat-and-monocle charm of Mr.
Peanut? The onomatopoetic panache of that snazzily gnomic triumvirate,
Snap, Crackle and Pop? And Mr. Clean says: "dependable power." The Curity
Nurse says: "comfort and ease." And Pinky the Salmon is leaping with our
happiness in mind. And the Pillsbury Dough Boy, homuncular, promising.
Tee and Eff, the Tastee Freeze ice cream sprites. The thousands of years of
vernal, panurgic clutter that thinly attends, but *does* attend, the Jolly Green
Giant, busy overseeing his demesne of fresh June peas. The Michelin Man
has survived since 1895. Perhaps the reigning bey of these winsome
schlockorama eidolons is yes, of course, Speedy Alka-Seltzer (effervescent
analgesic tablets "for relief")—with his hillock of carroty hair below the
tablet hat, with his wand, his wink, and a smile so sturdy it might be wielded
like a shield . . . who else could so hopefully lead us in battle against the
ravages of—remember Peter Pain? He looked like a pickle with three-day
stubble, with a troll's schnozzola, a thuggishly slanted gauchoesque hat, and
a cruel if miniature trident, for the implementing of "muscular aches and
pains." As if we need to be reminded that we live in the vale of woe and we

exit it dying, loss is writ in us as soon as the umbilicus is cut and from that moment never ceases, darkness blocks the way, our sicknesses can fit in a thimble but truncheon us to our knees, it's night, nobody cares enough or at all and a woman is curled to a monstrously diagnosed ball of hurting flesh in this poem, in this city, at any moment you think about human suffering, there's suffering.

5.

That night there's a "scene" in the bedroom. She
tells him. The "growth"—the fire—inside her is past all
masking over, and so she tells him. Not understanding
and understanding vie for control. She weeps, he
tells her their money will buy the best care possible.
Millions of years slip by, and finally they sleep
on a raft of exhaustion and mutual fright. That's
all: I won't reveal the long-term word from the lab.
What I want is studying them, where they're fit together
like soft tongs until morning; studying them, in their
unit-of-two unconsciousness and inarticulation; even
the rise of their chests is invisible now,
they could be a painting.

———

Yes, and
in the tacked-up print in the upstairs study, it's much
the same: the woman at the well
is singing—grief? or exultation? we don't know, but
singing, surely singing: in *her* world. For us,
outside of that plane, the room is silent,
dark now and silent, the woman is silent and still.

———

She
whaps the donkey's scabrous-yet-eloquent rump
—which right now signifies Animal Churlishness; and then they're
off, across the mallow dust of the plain, to the foothills.
The water jugs are stoppered and lashed to the pack-beast's ribby sides,
the sky is striped with cloud too thin to be anything
other than decoration . . . a day, an ordinary day
as it should be and usually is.
                              The priest
of the foothills is waiting at the cave-mouth. He's also
a mouth—that is, the Mountain God and the Bull God,
the Unutterable, the Tempering Flame and the Slayer of Infidels,
speaks through him: he wears the mask of a bull,
of beaten gold applied to cedar, as if to say the human medium

has been in contact intimate enough with the deific
to resemble it, as cast in human terms. He is one
of the "sensitives," one of the holy schizophrenics,
of his people. At night, he wanders from his body
through the abode of demons and guardian seraphs, only
a tendril of phlogistonic substance connecting him
back to his sleeping form; by day, he is known to fall
to the rockfloor like a man who's had his ankle-tendons severed,
and writhe there foaming, later to rise and deliver
the wisdoms of the Flame and Bull.
                                        And so she
is come for counsel: let's say a pain, let's say a mustard-grain
of pain, in her belly won't let her sleep, and what
does it mean? He stands in the smoke of the brazier,
the mask becoming even more life-like to her eyes.
It gleams — the Flame. He bellows — the Bull.
He bellows, he charges around the hill-floor crazily,
stumbling, smacking into the cave walls, overflowing
with his roar and gesturing wildly, like a hurt thing, like
a vessel touched by contents from a different world,
until even the far birds, even the stunted grasses, seem to her
to be symbolic of a level of Birds and Grasses
paradigmatic to ours . . . And then he drops, and cools and quiets, and
then repeats what he was told in his trance.
                                        The donkey,
even — she'd tethered it at a nearby bramble —
is braying, with the desperate edge of some *ubermatrix* message
to its simple yowl, a message larger than it is.

———

It's winter. Pipesmoke snow
skirtles over the blacktop.
The new moon's only a bone sherd
dug up out of the ungiving cold.
By now — how many poems do we need
to read, before we'll admit one thing

says another? that even the hummingbird skull,
the cigarette paper, the thumping cranberry heart
in the caked-over runt of the litter,
says another?

Nor is the initiation easy, into the shaman-like role of American Costumed Critter. "One contestant kept tripping over his Hula-Hoops. Another seemed dazed inside the costume, reeling like a top on its last spin. Another removed the Hugo head and vomited . . . " These failed acts are try-outs for a new Hugo the Hornet in Charlotte, North Carolina.

Every day, minimum wage or the glow of a Higher Calling beckons hundreds of Americans into becoming human-sized owls or collies or spritzerbottles of underarm deodorant (ambulatory, sequined, googoo-eyed) and parading the theme parks, astroturf, tv sets and neighborhood streets of this country.

There are, though, as Ned Zeman admits in *American Kabuki*, "pitfalls to walking through midtown Manhattan dressed as a giant white rabbit." Costumes can weigh up to 40 pounds. "Imagine that *and* oversize stuffed feet and hands and a head the size of a beer keg, a head that has no real eyes, allowing you to see only through a little hole in or near the mouth." The heat inside can be hellish (so can the odor of earlier occupants). And often enough, mosquitoes dervish circles through the head.

For those who demonstrate the Calling to Assume the Role—to be, not *don* but *be*, the hallowed Lotta Bull (roast beef) or Michaelangelo (a Teenage Mutant Ninja Turtle) or Dottie Drop (a glistered bead for the city water monopoly)—these hazards are only further spurs toward epiphany. This is the beauty part. "It's what I was put on this earth to do," says the man inside Cocky the Gamecock, "It's a gift." A man inside Bugs Bunny: "After a lot of practice, it all clicks. *You actually become the rabbit.*" A voice from out of the lime-green shag-rug megaphone-snouted body of the Phillie Phanatic: "It's what I am."

Whole stadiumsfull stand cheering with the synchronized rise of hackles. Grandmas let go their crutches, accept a rubber paw, and boogie. Toddlers fasten themselves to carpeted legs and, out of love, like any of us, refuse to let go. The wish of dying 7-year-olds is often to spend a day with such as these, the roosters and alligators and frolicsome mice of an alternate Earth where *comic* and *karmic* are wedded as one.

"Explains the Chicken, 'I want the Chicken to supersede the man.'"

———

She can't sleep. Much too much
floods in. Amid it all, she remembers
holding the boy to her shoulder once, at a parade;
he was as easy to hold as . . . the jug in that picture
up in the study. Captain Cosmo rode by
in his Cosmobile, the boy liked that. And,
near the end, not so important a figure
as all of the various Mickeys and Goofies,
Mr. Light-Brite slowly rolled past on a float of tinfoil wattage.
"Look," she'd said, "from Daddy's office."
The boy didn't care at all. But she,
refusing to think of safety in terms of money,
could think it as "Yes,
he'll protect us."

6.

And the battle is fought in the filamental flash
up someone's nerve-connected dyed-to-match
prosthetic hook-of-a-hand; in the shoptalk of light
and leaf sugars; the battle is on our bedsheets, is
in gamma rays, is sifting through the charged ennui
of the video-games arcade . . .
                                    the battle of wholeness
versus flying apart, the battle of the universe itself,
and of its planisphere: the beermug rings and their
shotglass moons, complexly staining a bar top.

———————

A hush falls over the mallow dust of the plain.

———————

And then he awoke, and arose, and smote his keepers,
and like the reeds of the waters he broke his chains,
and unto him called his (plague)mates
Weal and Woe, and then did he walk the lands
of the people once more, P-t-r Pain
        for I shall fear him, I dread his (evil eye) (?)
And then did he seek out conquest
        I shall fear him, I dread his green step
P-t-r Pain, the in-my-bowels-the-stabber
P-t-r Pain, the in-my-chest-a-jackal / (lion) (?)
Up is down, and every hand is turned against another
And then there was no safety for the people
from his three-prong-lance
        for I shall fear his three-prong-lance

And then did the cries rise up, and the people
beseeched. And it was heard; and from
the central plain, and thereupon the temple
of the central plain,* did Spee-d-Alka stride forth
with the Tablets of Relief

———————

*Scholars currently believe this was the Miles Laboratories, Inc., in Elkhart, Indiana,
where a statue to Spee-d-Alka (sometimes Alka Sel-T'zer) was honored.

115

it is ours to swallow (? see "ingest")
with works-like-magic
   praise him
   it is ours to take as directed
Spee-d-Alka who rallies the forces that stay our anguish.

Then did the battle ensue.

––––––––

It's summer. The air is smeared with summer,
the drone of the bees is a fat sound, and the long day thins
away like trickled butter over the lake.
                        The waves
are involved in the project the rows of aspen boughs
continue: trans /
                        substantiating the light, into another
one of the fragmented bodies of Earth.
                        And
the flowers close, and the awnings furl,
and the alley becomes a lushly-stocked thesaurus
read by the whiskers of rats.
                        Everywhere,
the intangible is verified through its messengers.
The stars speak spectra. Moses
understood the announcement out of the bush.

––––––––

The prayer is the same in any language:
Thank you. Help me. Look upon
our plight and daily striving, Absolute of Absolutes,
and rain down armies of Your fierce and invincible Righteous Enablement.
Heal us.

––––––––

And thus did Alka make war on Pain, and
(here the script breaks off)

The battle is daily waged, the cosmic battle
of Order versus Entropy

If you would deny it
a place at our table

try telling this woman curled in her bed despairing
tell the biopsy slide

7.

"The Reverend Patrick Brontë, wishing to know more about the minds of his
six motherless children than he had hitherto discovered, placed each one
behind a mask to make them speak with less timidity than before . . . "

I've turned to watch her undone face in sleep
become the spokesface

for the morphic fields of sentient life
in the air, for the presto-chango
physics of void and matter, of matter and void,
and for the lovely broken contiguity
of mind and flesh . . .

and needed to kiss it halfway wakeful, back
again into being her face.

———

The house was charged with . . . he didn't know
what, he was four. He was four and
awake in the gravid darkness.
This had happened before, and he knew what to do
to quiet himself: he went to the upstairs study
and turned on the light there. This was his father's room,
the light was Mr. Light-Brite most
especially here, a personal, watchful light.
And even at four he wasn't immune to the sexual
stamina held in check in the skin of the woman
at the well—the way her simple gown was shadowed
at an angle from her hip-swell to the lifted vessel,
over her breasts. And in the silence
he can hear, or sense the possiblity to hear,
that world—to hear,
not the clay, but the crystalline grid
in clay, not the donkey, the Donkey,
the prototypical wail, the first condensing gas
this plain of mallow dust with its grief and brief pleasures
descended from in the time before time,

and was mixed to an iffy stability with the spit of stars
and baked to crazing under our own relentless sun, and
now out of the mouth of clay pours forth the water;

and out of the woman, a song.

Lullabye

Lullabye

sleep, little beansprout
don't be scared
the night is simply the true sky
bared

sleep, little dillseed
don't be afraid
the moon is the sunlight
ricocheted

sleep, little button
don't make a fuss
we make up the gods
so they can make us

sleep, little nubbin
don't you stir
this sky smiled down
on Atlantis and Ur

NOTES

"*Shoyn Fergéssin*: 'I've Forgotten' in Yiddish": The charming second part of this poem's melting-pot joke: Another man speaks up, "That's my name too." "You? You're Chinese!" "That's right. I was behind this other guy in line" (pointing) "and when they asked for my name I said *Sam Ting*."

"The Jewish Poets of Arabic Spain . . . ": I am indebted (despite my meddlesome rearranging of their materials) to *The Jewish Poets of Spain* (David Goldstein) and *Sunflower Splendor: Three Thousand Years of Chinese Poetry* (Wu-Chi Liu and Irving Yucheng Lo).

"Will the Real Shakespeare Please Stand Up?" is dedicated to Helen Brewer.

"Stories": *bris*, circumcision; *mohel*, circumciser

"The Book of Speedy": In a few places this poem relies on the texts of others, although quoted material is sometimes reworded from its original source for my purposes. I must gratefully acknowledge Russell Hoban (the memory of the tethered donkey), Richard Attenborough (on Tiki gods), Ned Zeman (performers in character costume), and Daphne du Maurier (the Brontë family).